CALLED ALONGSIDE:

Essays by Pastor's Wives for Pastor's Wives

Edited by
Gary L. Shultz Jr.

Copyright Page

Copyright © 2025 Gary Lee Shultz Jr. All rights reserved.

"Scripture quotations taken from the New American Standard Bible®, Copyright © 1960, 1962, 1963, 1968, 1971, 1972, 1973, 1975, 1977, 1995 by The Lockman Foundation Used by permission." (www.Lockman.org)

Baptist University Press

5400 College Dr.

Graceville, FL 32440

www.bup.buf.edu

ISBN

DEDICATION

To Kristin, pastor's wife to Pleasant View Baptist Church; First Baptist Church Fulton, MO; First Baptist Church Tallahassee, FL; and Thomas Memorial Baptist Church.

TABLE OF CONTENTS

Foreword 7
Clayton Cloer

Introduction 9
Gary L. Shultz Jr.

Satan's Lies to Ministers' Wives 12
Liz Traylor

All Things New: When the Pastor's Wife is a First-Generation Christian 27
Seana Reavis

Pouring from an Empty Cup: Soul Care for the Ministry Wife 40
Jennifer Gaddis

Making Friends is Always Worth It 51
Tiffany Burgner

Today Years Old 56
Monique N. Igbinoba-Cummings

Two Callings, One Covenant: Tending the Garden Together 65
Jennifer Duncan

The Biblical Calling of the Pastor's Wife 75
Gary L. Shultz Jr.

List of Contributors 89

FOREWORD

"Who can find a virtuous wife? For her worth is far above rubies" (Proverbs 31:10). "Virtuous" translates the Hebrew word used for the valor and courage of a warrior. A pastor's wife possesses more courage than most. She processes all the complexity, rigor, challenges, and tragedies that her husband addresses. The pastor's wife holds a high and holy place in the ministry of the church. Her character, class, and grace grants the congregation an inspiring example to follow. In most contexts, the pastor's wife shepherds the ladies in the church.

Some years ago, I was invited to lead a pastor's conference in Tanzania in a remote area without running water. The pastors and their families traveled in to the location from one province. We studied the word all day and held evangelistic meetings in the evenings. The pastors' wives took care of the children, fixed the food for the conference, and studied together with an amazing teacher. I would stand under a building without air conditioning and look out the window while teaching. I watched a pastor's wife take care of a newborn, an 18-month-old, and a three-year-old while scalding a chicken and listening to every translated word that I was saying. These ladies prepared the lunch and dinner for all of us while educating the children and listening to the teaching. In the afternoons, the children would be put down for a nap and I would instruct the entire group. Those wives and mothers displayed such humility, work ethic, patience, and grace. The pastors inspired me that week, but their wives moved me to tears.

I can speak from personal experience about the power, beauty, and virtue of a Holy Spirit filled pastor's wife. When I married Linda 35 years ago, she stood at the alter with a young businessman with a well-planned career in front of him. Two and half years later, God called me into the ministry. For more than 30 years, I have been shaped and strengthened by the wisdom, integrity, faithfulness, and virtue of Linda. God changed my ministry and my life through her influence. I have seen her navigate the most complex relationships and undefined responsibilities. She has endured various unjust situations and circumstances. She would tell you that her life has been filled with joyful seasons in the home, in the church, and in the university setting. I may be the head of our home, but she is the heart. Her worth is far above rubies. It is immeasurable.

In an age of aspiring to be at the top, demanding rights, and seeking promotion, pastors' wives are humble, faithful, courageous, and clothed in beauty. This book speaks from the incredible experience of some of the most underappreciated ladies in our churches, the pastors' wives. As you read these essays, I trust that you will be moved and blessed.

Clayton Cloer
President
Baptist University of Florida

INTRODUCTION
Gary L. Shultz Jr.

When a married man is called into pastoral ministry, his wife is called into ministry alongside him. This is true regardless of her circumstances. No matter her age, career, background, education, gifts, talents, personality, number of children, whether the children are still in the home or not, whether she works outside the home or not, or any other circumstance, when God calls a woman's husband into vocational ministry, he calls her into ministry as well.[1]

This is also true regardless of the church and the structure of the church. Some churches (or church members) recognize this calling, others do not. Some churches have one pastor, some churches have a senior pastor with one or more associate pastors, some churches have multiple pastors serving on a pastoral board together. Some churches go out of their way to emphasize that a pastor's wife is just another church member, some churches have clear expectations of a pastor's wife, some churches have unspoken (but still just as serious!)

---

[1] Of course, the reverse is also true. If a married woman is called into vocational ministry, her husband is called into a particular type of ministry alongside her as well. However, the focus of this book is on the unique role of pastor's wife. All the authors in this book write serve in the context of the Southern Baptist Convention, with the conviction that only men should serve as pastors. See Article VI of the Baptist Faith and Message 2000, available at https://bfm.sbc.net/bfm2000/#vi.

INTRODUCTION

expectations of a pastor's wife. Whichever kind of church a pastor's wife might find herself in, God's calling persists.

As with all his callings, God intends the call of a pastor's wife to be a blessing. Too often, however, it can be burdensome, frustrating, lonely, misunderstood, discouraging, or all of these put together. There is no explanation of this call in Scripture as there is for the pastor (though as we shall see, that doesn't mean Scripture is completely silent about it). Churches don't typically hire and pay their pastors' wives to be pastor's wives. Even churches with clear expectations for their pastor's wife don't typically write them down or plainly state them for her as they would for her husband. Juggling the responsibilities of family, church, career, and a personal relationship with God is never easy. Churches and church members can be difficult. Marriages can be better or worse. And sometimes, the burdens and discouragement are self-imposed, the result of particular seasons of life, unique times of suffering, or "dry times" with God.

The purpose of this book is to encourage you, the pastor's wife, in your calling alongside your husband. To accomplish that, we've included seven essays in this book. The first six essays are written by current pastor's wives, serving throughout the state of Florida in different churches and ministry contexts. Each author reflects on their experiences, callings, and Scripture to help you not only to endure, but to thrive in your unique calling.

Liz Traylor surveys fifty pastor's wives and responds to some of the lies Satan loves to tell pastor's wives, redirecting us to the promises and instruction of Scripture.

Seana Reavis reflects on her experience as a first-generation Christian serving as a pastor's wife, offering encouragement to those who might find themselves in a similar situation.

Jennifer Gaddis focuses on soul care for the pastor's wife, recommending several practices that will help you thrive before God in your calling.

Tiffany Burgner exhorts pastors' wives to make and keep friends in the church as a part of their calling, even when it is hard, because the blessings God brings through these relationships are always worth it.

Monique Igbinoba-Cummings looks back at her experience of beginning her role as pastor's wife with obvious expectations but no clear direction, offering counsel and encouragement for every pastor's wife's journey.

Jennifer Duncan considers how God works in and through the pastor's wife when she is also called to vocational ministry, using the metaphor of tending a garden to contemplate how God blesses in these circumstances.

Finally, in the last essay, I offer my reflections on what the Bible does tell us about this wonderful calling, exploring the biblical understanding of this call and how the Bible guides pastors' wives in fulfilling it.

Pastor's wives, please know I'm thankful for each one of you and how you pour your life into your family, your husband, your church, your calling, and your relationship with God. My prayer for you as you read this book is that you would be deeply encouraged to "press on toward the goal for the prize of the upward call of God in Christ Jesus" (Phil 3:14).

SATAN'S LIES TO MINISTERS' WIVES
Liz Traylor

Satan began shooting his fiery darts at me on the second date with the man I would eventually marry. He was a college senior, already pastoring a church, and I knew I didn't want to be a preacher's wife. I had vivid, pre-conceived notions of what life was like in the ministry. I'd have to wear skirts all the time. I'd have to move every three years. I would be in charge of women's ministry. And, of course, I'd have to play the piano.

He (my now-husband) had already queried, "If I were to ask you The Question, do you know what you would say?" He wasn't going to propose without knowing my answer because he doesn't like to lose. I didn't know, so I was honest and said so. I had to make sure I was doing the right thing because I was not going to demoralize his pastorate or ruin his life.

The most efficient way to derail a man's ministry is to end his marriage, and the easiest way to cause him strife is to have a wife who is miserable all the time. Therefore, the devil goes to work on wives as only he can. We must continually be on guard because he lies to all of us when and where we are the weakest.

I surveyed fifty wives of ministry leaders and asked them, "What is Satan's number one lie to minsters' wives?" The answers were varied, but they can be consolidated into ten responses.

1. You've given up everything for God and that makes you special.

I planned to marry a man with dark hair who loved ballroom dancing and who would build me one house I could live in for the rest of my life. Instead, I married a red-haired pastor with no fancy footwork except as quarterback on the football field. We've lived in three states and in seven homes.

One day, even though I loved my spouse, I asked God why he hadn't given me what was on my "potential husband" list. After all, Psalm 37:4 says, "Delight yourself in the Lord, and He will give you the desires of your heart." The Lord responded:

- You didn't ask me before you made the list.
- I alone know what you need.
- You had to learn to delight in me.
- I changed your heart's desires.

I realized he truly had altered everything, and what I had given up really didn't matter. I got what I needed: security. Wherever we went, God was there before us. Whatever we faced, I knew He would fight our battles. Wherever he moved us became our home.

God gave up his Son, Jesus gave up His life, and we are special solely because we are created by the Almighty. "Look what I have done for God" only resonates with selfish people.

Don't listen to the lie. Read 1 Samuel 15:22 "Samuel said, 'Has the LORD as much delight in burnt offerings and sacrifices as in obeying the voice of the LORD? Behold, to obey is better than sacrifice, and to heed than the fat of rams."

2. Your husband's relationship to God is sufficient for you both.

For our first thirteen years of marriage, I hoped this was true. Although I had a salvation experience, my spiritual growth ended there. I didn't read the Bible or pray regularly until I was diagnosed with textbook clinical burnout. My counselor sent me home to do nothing but rest for two weeks, so I decided I might as well read Scripture. I began in Mark simply because it is the shortest gospel, and I was astounded by the Jesus I met there. He was so much more than Sunday School Jesus I had learned about growing up.

I began writing down my prayers in a notebook. The fourteen days of time with God expanded to four weeks, then four months, and then forever. Since then, very few mornings have gone by when I have not spent quality time with the Lord. I learned I am nothing without him, that I cannot survive without him—especially in the ministry.

You must have your own personal relationship with the Savior. You must read his Word for yourself. You must spend time with God in prayer. Only then can you thrive in your marriage and ministry.

Don't listen to the lie. Read Matthew 22:37-39. "And He said to him, 'YOU SHALL LOVE THE LORD YOUR GOD WITH ALL YOUR HEART, AND WITH ALL YOUR SOUL, AND WITH ALL YOUR MIND. This is the great and foremost commandment. The second is like it, YOU SHALL LOVE YOUR NEIGHBOR AS YOURSELF.'"

3. You must be at church every time the doors open.

I never told our children they had to go to church and be part of all the activities because their father was the pastor. I taught them we go to church because we love God. We need to learn more about him in small group, be part of corporate worship, and fellowship with other believers.

However, we often over-program our churches, and though we may feel obligated, we must be realistic. We have limited energy. We are in different seasons of our lives. We have different interests and abilities. For example, our daughter adored choir, but because singing was equivalent to torture to our musically-challenged son, he was not required to participate.

There is a higher standard for the minister's family, but there were some Sunday nights when our children needed downtime after a stressful week and required a good night's sleep for school the next day. Dad went on to church, but we stayed home. I'm sure there were church members who didn't approve, but I do not ultimately answer to them. Only to God.

Don't listen to the lie. Read Mark 6:31. "And He said to them, 'Come away by yourselves to a secluded place and rest a while.'"

4. If you don't do it, it won't get done.

Whatever "it" is, it never gets finished—especially at church. There will always be a class that needs a teacher, a group that needs a leader, or a committee that needs more workers. But do I have to take on an activity when it is outside my spiritual giftedness and the calling of God? No.

What does the Lord require of me? "He has told you, O man, what is good; and what does the LORD require of you but to do justice, to love kindness, and to walk humbly with your God?" (Micah 6:8). Not a word about organizing a retreat, entertaining deacons' wives, or singing in the choir.

Nothing should be accomplished at the expense of your relationship with God. Only when I can hear the prompting of the Holy Spirit can I do what He says to do. Then, even though serving within God's call can be difficult, it is a burden that is light.

Jesus had been teaching people all day and could have kept on telling parable after parable, yet he left the crowds, got in a boat, took a nap, stilled a storm, and crossed to the other side of the Sea of Galilee. He knew he needed to walk away and recuperate his strength.

Since Jesus acknowledged his human limits, so should I. I've learned to:

- Set my priorities: God, husband, family, church
- Simplify my life: what I have, what I do, where I go
- Schedule my rest: get enough sleep, relax, and breathe deeply
- Keep my expectations low: I will never be perfect
- Keep my goals attainable: my house is clean enough
- Keep my aspirations high: be like Jesus

Don't listen to the lie. Read Mark 4:35-36. "On that day, when evening came, He said to them, 'Let us go over to the other side.' Leaving the crowd, they took Him along with them in the boat, just as He was; and other boats were with Him."

5. Your children must be perfect, or your husband's ministry will suffer.

Your children will be normal, and most people will breathe a sigh of relief. Both our children were considered "good kids," yet they were very independent and came with individual challenges to our parenting ability.

Our son was especially curious and full of energy. When he was four years old, he pulled the fire alarm our first night at the new church. A few years later, three people came to me over the course of one Sunday evening to tell me he was outside jumping up and down on top of our Suburban, he was straddling the balcony rail like he was riding a horse, and he was spitting off the balcony. Each time I responded, "Thank you very much." I didn't punish him for acting like any other boy in church, but we did have an interesting discussion on the way home.

When he was in college, one of those informers stopped me in the worship center and said, "I need to tell you something. When Bennett was little, I didn't approve of the way you raised him. But he's turned into a fine young man."

Many years have passed, and our children and their families are in church each week. They are rearing our grandchildren "in the discipline and instruction of the Lord" (Eph 6:4). God has given us everything we need for life and godliness. Read his word. Ask him for guidance. He knows your children and can tell you exactly how to be the parent they need—no matter what other people think.

Don't listen to the lie. Read 2 Peter 1:3. "Seeing that His divine power has granted to us everything pertaining to life and godliness, through the true knowledge of Him who called us by His own glory and excellence."

6. You must do your best to please everyone because they are watching you.

Yes, people are watching you everywhere you go. However, pleasing everyone is impossible. Even Jesus and John the Baptist couldn't do it. Jesus said: "John came neither eating nor drinking, and they say, 'He has a demon!' The Son of Man came eating and drinking, and they say, 'Behold a gluttonous man and a drunkard, a friend of tax-gatherers and sinners!' (Matt 11:18-19)." And those were probably church people talking.

I've known ministers' wives who were shy and reserved, outgoing and social, brilliant and introverted, and fun-loving and talkative. They have been stay-at-home moms, schoolteachers, business owners, financial planners, research chemists, and trauma nurses. Some were up-front leaders, and some were behind-the-scenes servants. All of them were more than likely criticized by someone at least once during their ministries.

No matter who we are or what we do, we must always be genuine and real—the women God made in His own image. Before I walk out the door, I make sure my inward attitude is pleasing to God and my heart is pure before Him. Then I look in the mirror, check my outward appearance, and ask God, "Do I in any way dishonor my Lord, my spouse, or my church?" If I feel His approval inside and out, that is enough.

Don't listen to the lie. Read 1 Timothy 2:9-10. "Likewise, I want women to adorn themselves with proper clothing, modestly and discreetly, not with braided hair and gold or pearls or costly garments, but rather by means of good works, as is proper for women making a claim to godliness."

7. You cannot have close friends who are members of your church.

Jesus had an elite group within the apostles (Peter, James, and John) and the other nine seemed to understand. We, too, should be able to have close friends in church, but choose them with care. Be cautious and prayerful, proceed slowly, and ask God for clear discernment.

Ask yourself:

- Do they want to be my friend only for the prestige of knowing the minister's wife?

- Are they attempting to influence my husband through me?

- Are they looking for the inside scoop—the gossip—to spread as "prayer requests?"

- Are they trustworthy, godly women?

Three women in my church have been my friends for the past thirty years. We all serve in vastly different ministries and are careful not to flaunt our friendship at church. Though we only meet to fellowship several times a year, we stay in close contact and are prayer warriors for each other. We have prayed our way through breast cancer, the birth of grandchildren, the death of an adult child, and caregiving for our aging parents. God gave me a treasure when he gave me their love and support. But I still don't tell them everything I know about church, and they never hear me complain about their pastor.

I have one church member friend who has proven her confidence over the years. I call her my "iron sharpens iron friend" (Prov 27:17), because she will always tell me the truth. But I still don't tell her the deepest secrets of my heart.

Only Jesus knows me. He is the friend who is always faithful and "sticks closer than a brother" (Prov 18:24). One of my favorite hymns is "What a Friend We Have in Jesus." The opening line is, "What a friend we have in Jesus, all our sins and griefs to bear; what a privilege to carry everything to God in prayer." I can tell him anything because he already knows it all. Make sure your very best friend is Jesus.

Don't listen to the lie. Read 1 Corinthians 1:9. "God is faithful, through whom you were called into fellowship with His Son, Jesus Christ our Lord."

8. No other wife's husband is gone as much, works as hard, or is busy as yours.

Try saying that to the wives of deployed military personnel, airline pilots, professional baseball players, and evangelists I have known. But this is still the lie I fall prey to most often. If I'm not diligent, I find myself singing, "Nobody knows the trouble I've seen," over and over until I'm filled with self-pity.

Yes, our husbands are gone a lot, always on call, and way too busy. Often most of the child-rearing falls on us. But ministry is his calling, his occupation, his job, and we must understand that with leadership comes added responsibilities.

However, sometimes our husbands get caught up in the needs of the church to the neglect of their wives and families. That's exactly what happened to us. One night I was so exasperated, I looked at my husband and said, "You don't even like our children, do you?" He turned and walked out of the house to go to deacons' meeting without saying a word.

I started "prayer complaining" to God. "Lord, I can't do this anymore! He had better start spending time with his kids or they will never have a relationship with him when they grow up. I'm going to tell him what...." Before I finished the sentence I heard the Spirit whisper in my heart, "Close your mouth."

"But if I don't tell him, he won't know what he is doing wrong." Again, in a louder voice this time, "Close your mouth." Then I had the audacity to say, "But God...." And I heard the definitive response: "CLOSE YOUR MOUTH." I had a choice to make. I could be obedient or keep talking. I chose to be obedient, except to beg God to do something quickly because I wouldn't last long in the current situation.

I would love to tell you everything was perfect after that, but the next several weeks were miserable. Stress and frustration abounded as the evil one tried to deepen the rift between us, but I was victorious and kept my mouth shut.

The following Sunday, my husband closed the service by telling the congregation he would be preaching a series from Malachi. My jaw dropped. I knew the last verse of the book: God would "turn the hearts of the fathers to their children and the hearts of children to their fathers" (Mal 4:6).

The next week he referred to a parenting book someone had sent him. He choked up as he declared, "I never met a man in prison who loved his father." Over the following months, I watched God change my husband's heart, and I watched my husband reprioritize his schedule. I never mentioned parenting advice to him again, and I praised God for the miracles only he could perform.

Don't listen to the lie. Read Exodus 14:14. "The LORD will fight for you while you keep silent."

9. Nobody understands what you are going through.

Sometimes I'm frustrated because my husband doesn't even understand what I am experiencing, but then he's never been a minister's wife, has he? I shouldn't be surprised by his lack of empathy. While no one understands my specific situations, myriads of staff wives have experienced the same challenges. Many of them have had much worse scenarios to deal with than I have. I need their advice and camaraderie.

It is important to build a network of women from whom I can learn and commiserate. I know God hears and understands, but as one of our church preschoolers wailed, "I need someone with skin on them!"

Find a mentor in an older pastor's wife who has finished well. Spend time with her, ask her questions, listen to her stories, and absorb her wisdom. Ask, "What would you do differently if you had it all to do over, but with the knowledge you have now?"

If you are in a church with multiple staff members, get to know the wives. As pastor's wife, I began with monthly meetings but quickly found that was too much for everyone's schedules. Now we try to meet for dinner or prayer several times a year. The most effective fellowship we have is a catered staff and family lunch right after church. We are already there, so the gathering is convenient for everyone, and wives appreciate not having to prepare lunch for their families.

Attend ministry wives' events when they are available in your area or reach out and meet some wives on your own. Others are struggling with issues, too, and you can share your burdens and pray for each other. Social media platforms are now available with information, help, support groups, and a variety of ways to connect with other ministry wives. There are plenty of women who *do* understand what you are going through. You just have to take the initiative to find them.

Don't listen to the lie. Read 1 Thessalonians 5:11. "Therefore encourage one another and build up one another, just as you also are doing."

10. If you can just move to a new church, you'll be happy.

Moving never solved my problems. In fact, I've found three things to be true in all the churches my husband has pastored.

1. The people may have different names, but the personalities are the same everywhere you go. No matter the size, location, or age of the church, you will find smiling manipulators, hypocritical grumblers, underhanded troublemakers, and unsaved church members. You will also meet mighty people of faith and gentle servants of Jesus. Spend time with those precious saints of God.

2. If the problem is you, the problem goes with you wherever you go. If you need to admit you are a minister's wife who has never committed her life to Christ, repent and be saved. If you need the infilling of the Holy Spirit, remove whatever quenches or grieves him in your life. If you need help for a mental health issue, seek a Christian counselor. But for some of us, we simply need an attitude adjustment. Expressing gratefulness to Almighty God usually cures me of my whining.

3. The next church may be even more of a challenge, and I write that from real life experience. Before we moved in 1990 to the church we still serve, we had never faced angry church members. But that all changed six years later when a small group decided it was time for us to go. I learned more about

God and his amazing provision for me when I thought I couldn't stand another day in ministry.

We know the verse, "I can do all things through Him who strengthens me" (Phil 4:13), but we usually quote and apply it totally out of context. In the preceding verses, Paul writes that he knows how to get along with very little and how to live in prosperity. He has learned the secret of being well fed and going hungry, living in abundance or suffering need. That secret is not in being happy, but in being content.

Note that Paul wrote he has learned the secret. It didn't come naturally. He gained that knowledge because God strengthened him in every circumstance. God will be our strength when we learn to be content right where we are.

Don't listen to the lie. Read 2 Corinthians 12:9. "And He has said to me, 'My grace is sufficient for you, for power is perfected in weakness.' Most gladly, therefore, I will rather boast about my weaknesses, so that the power of Christ may dwell in me."

CONCLUSION

Remember, there is only one enemy—and it is not your church. God clearly shows us in his Word how to defeat the evil one.

First, **KNOW HIS SCHEMES**. Watch for them. Be wary of them. Paul stated, "We are not ignorant of his schemes" (2 Cor 2:11).

He tempts us where we are weakest. He tempts us to do what is contrary to God's will. He tempts us with "the lust of the flesh, the lust of the eyes, and the boastful pride of life" (1 John 2:16).

He deceives us as an "angel of light" (2 Cor 11:14). His servants, false apostles and deceitful workers, disguise themselves as servants of righteousness and followers of Christ (2 Cor 11:13,15). Train your senses to discern good from evil (Heb 5:14).

He roars like a lion. "Your adversary, the devil, prowls around like a roaring lion, seeking someone to devour" (1 Pet 5:8-9). The word "like" is a simile, a comparison. Only Jesus is the Lion of Judah. Satan is loud. The Spirit speaks in "a still small voice" (1 Kings 19:12 KJV). We have to hush to hear him.

To defeat Satan's schemes, we must **RECOGNIZE HIS LIES**. Don't be gullible. Don't believe everything that enters your mind. Weigh your decisions next to Scripture and make your decisions after prayer. "He is a liar and the father of lies" (John 8:44)

He offers compromises in our spiritual journeys. "I have peace though I walk in the stubbornness of my heart" (Deut 29:19-20) is a terrifying belief system. "I know this is a sin, but I'll just ask God to forgive me" doesn't work. Half obedience is full disobedience. There are no compromises with God.

He distorts the truth. Satan distorted God's commands to Eve, and he is still twisting truth today. He sounds logical—*you deserve this*. He sounds subtle—*no one will know*. He sounds sincere—*God will understand*. The real truth is Jesus (John 10:10).

He is the accuser of us all, and guilt is his number one tool against women. He declares, "How can God use you when you failed Him so miserably?" In response, recite biblical examples of forgiven believers back to him. He argues, "Are you sure God has forgiven you?" If you truly repented, trust you are forgiven and forgive yourself. Don't fall for his schemes.

We can **ASSURE HIS DEFEAT**. We can overcome the evil one (1 John 2:14). Jesus has "rendered powerless...the devil" (Heb 2:14). To make him powerless in our lives requires sanctification. We must study, memorize, and quote the Word of God back to Satan just as Jesus did. We must follow God's precepts and commands and "not give the devil an opportunity" (Eph 4:27) in any area of our lives. We must "walk in the Spirit" (Gal 5:16) so we do not gratify the flesh.

Sometimes we are told to turn and run—from the sins of monetary obsession (1 Tim 6:9-10), youthful lusts (2 Tim 2:22), and sexual immorality (1 Cor6:18). Sometimes we must stand and fight. Rebuke him (Matt 16:23), resist him (James 4:7), and put on the armor of God (Eph 6:11). Only then can we guarantee the defeat of the enemy as we fulfill our calling as ministers' wives.

A few weeks after my husband asked me if I had an answer for The Question, God called me to be a pastor's wife in a very clear and definitive way. I walked up and announced, "When you are ready to ask me to marry you, the answer is yes." I was not prepared for what lay ahead, but I was sure I was doing the right thing. After almost fifty years, I am still sure—and still rebuking Satan's lies to this minister's wife.

ALL THINGS NEW:
When the Pastor's Wife is a First-Generation Christian
Seana Reavis

There are pastor's wives who, as young girls, grew up in pastor's or ministry leader's homes. There are also pastor's wives who did not grow up with parents in ministry, but their homes were led by godly Christians who served in their local church. There are pastor's wives whose childhoods were not spent in Christ-centered households, but instead in homes of hypocritical Christian parents. Then there are pastor's wives who grew up in homes in which Christianity was not professed at all. Finally, there are pastor's wives who grew up in broken homes, rough places where lostness was obvious. I fall hard into the last category, but it is my joy to testify that God calls pastors and their wives from myriad backgrounds and has good purposes for them all!

I became a Christian in high school, after two Christian classmates invited me to visit their church with them. My family seldom attended worship services at any church, but I took my friends up on their offer to ride with their families to their church because I was curious. After responding to the gospel and calling on the Lord as my Savior, church became my favorite (and safest) place to be. Still, I never saw myself surrendering to ministry, and I never ever saw myself being a pastor's wife one day! Yet nearly 20 years ago, I married my soulmate, my pastor husband, clueless to what all was ahead of us. Today, I sit with gratitude as I reflect on some of the unique challenges and victories of being a first-generation Christian pastor's wife, and hopefully I can offer encouragement to anyone on that path!

Unique Challenges

"What is it like to be a pastor's wife?" Every pastor's wife that I have ever met has been asked this question. If the person asking is a Christian, then they can probably understand living (and sometimes being measured) by a higher standard in the eyes of a watching world. All pastor's wives live with higher expectations, in the eyes of a watching world *and* in the eyes of a watching church. The life of a pastor's wife is unique to say the least. It has unique challenges and headwinds, as well as unique graces and joys. For the pastor's wife that is a first-generation Christian, the headwinds can be broadly summed up as extra expectations, extra cluelessness, extra exposure, and extra loneliness.

Extra Expectations

A pastor's wife who is a first-generation Christian enters a life of maximum expectations with minimal support. She must learn how to be a godly wife and mother, in real time and in front of a live audience, for all the years that she serves at the church(es) that her husband shepherds. Nearly everything in her ministry life after her wedding day is likely new to her, and nearly everything she does in her ministry life is observed from her wedding day onward.

The level of difficulty (without even accounting for the type of church or cultural factors that carry massive daily impact) in the fishbowl of ministry compounds with each degree of separation from prior lived experience. It increases from being raised in ministry, to being raised in a lay Christian home, to then being raised in a merely moral home, all the way to being raised in a dysfunctional environment or even in outright depravity. A pastor's wife who was not raised in ministry but was raised in a godly home is at least able to follow a personal role model, although it is still a big adjustment to go from their childhood house to a glass house. Anyone already in ministry will confirm, and anyone heading into ministry will soon learn, that church leadership and church membership are related but immeasurably dissimilar. Still, while that pastor's wife will need to get comfortable with church ministry life, she is at least likely to already be comfortable with home life, unlike the first-generation Christian pastor's wife.

There is a greater level of wisdom, maturity, morality, and overall self-mastery that is typically presumed upon pastor's wives, regardless of how young or inexperienced she is. Everyone admits that no one is perfect, but the world would like to see Christians come the closest to hitting the mark, and pastor's wives even more. If this weren't already enough, a pastor's wife who did not have a godly upbringing bears the weight of added pressure to give all that she never received and to pursue the home life that she always dreamt of but has never experienced.

Extra Cluelessness

All these extra expectations stack tall against the lack of practice that she has had living in a Christ-centered home, let alone adding the demands of church ministry. A wife and mother that was raised by a truly Christian wife and mother has a template in her mind based on what was modeled in front of her for years. The floor plan for a gospel-proclaiming home is embedded in her mind and heart. She still relies on the instructions of Scripture, but the precepts fit neatly with what she saw and felt growing up. The Christian wife and mother that was not raised like the former has the same biblical instructions and materials for a gospel home set before her, but she's never actually seen anyone build this particular floor plan. Building a new house is a huge undertaking for anyone, but someone who has first watched their parent(s) display how to do it well at least knows it is doable.

For a first-generation Christian woman, the start of her married life can feel like facing a towering pile of building materials with a thick manual in hand, being tasked to build a house from scratch, yet clueless of where or how to even begin. If she comes from a dysfunctional home, add confusion to cluelessness as the mission now grows to include unlearning all the harmful choices that can damage or destroy a house. It's the difference between the confidence you feel when preparing a recipe that you've seen and done multiple times before versus working through a complicated new recipe. Every step feels like it takes twice as long as you check back and forth between the instructions and your progress, second-guessing yourself most of the time, and doubting that what you produce will look anything like what you desperately hope for. We all must learn in marriage and motherhood, but some of us must learn more in a shorter time. The pastor's wife who is a first-generation Christian can feel behind, out of place, out of sync, and often bewildered and overwhelmed (if not self-conscious) at best. Everything feels harder.

Extra Exposure

Try as she might to care only that God is watching, the first-generation Christian who is also a pastor's wife does all of this in front of an audience that includes the church she serves. Learning something new under observation is a special kind of discomfort, as there's no exposure quite like being made an example for all to see. Making it even harder is that despite the constant scrutiny, ministry might be the one field where describing the vocational challenges is often interpreted as complaining, especially for a woman. We are meant to be so humbly grateful for our calling and so spiritually mature that we're miraculously ready to take on the new homebuilding process unaffected by our roots, and to welcome the spectators while we're at it.

The final challenge to all these headwinds is perhaps the hardest. A pastor's wife who is a first-generation Christian usually does not have the support of her childhood family to encourage her to create a family that is different from the one of her childhood. Moreover, since she's expected to immediately step into the role of the "professional Christian wife and mother" for her church family regardless of her inexperience, she often doesn't have the freedom to share the obstacles that she faces. Church leadership is a relatively lonely role already, but the first-generation Christian pastor's wife can feel utterly alone except for the constant company of expectations, cluelessness, and public exposure.

Unique Victories

Ironically, at the start of ministry I ignorantly anticipated that ministry would be the most peaceful and pleasant vocation. I was so accustomed to drama and trauma through childhood that I looked forward to spending my adulthood in the relative bliss of ministry life, full of joyful corporate worship and fellowship. While there is much joyful worship and fellowship, there is also much grief and pain. I quickly realized that ministry life was not an escape from drama and trauma, but would instead place my husband and I near everyone else's drama and trauma daily. Moreover, there is a tendency for church members to assume that the lives of those in ministry are insulated from life's usual hassles and hardships. Your unlimited availability is frequently expected. Seldom do people realize that those serving in ministry bear the weight of their own concerns and struggles (both past and present) along with those of their church members. Now, I must say that while it is tempting to see the life of a first-generation pastor's wife as one of all pressure and no preparation for her ministry, please rest assured it is true that God equips those he calls. The equipping may come from Bible college or seminary, from your personal discipleship, and even from your past experiences.

Grace

Biblically, the two most important priorities for a woman after her personal relationship with God are her relationship with her husband and her relationship with her children. So, the first-generation Christian woman's top three priorities in life are the top three things that she wasn't taught to prioritize growing up: God, godly marriage, and godly motherhood. I remember feeling overwhelmed that the most important things I held in my life were the very things that I understood the least about what to do with.

I now look back and thank God for that salient feeling of inadequacy, or else I might have defaulted to self-reliance if I had thought I knew what I was doing. An upside of family life for a first-generation Christian woman is that she's not really surprised when things go awry as much as she is when things turn out well. She has low expectations for things to go well, so when they do, she has even more reason to credit the grace of God because it certainly couldn't have been her instincts. I feel desperate for God's grace in my marriage, motherhood, and ministry most days. I used to feel frustration on top of it all for needing God's help in every single household task, from the most menial to monumental. But why be frustrated by an awareness of the state of dependence that Scripture emphasizes that *every* believer should embrace *every* day? We are *all* deficient, regardless of breeding and background. Our only hope is the one sufficient Redeemer who has transferred us into his forever family. None of us are ever enough, but

God's grace is more than enough to work in and through us by the power of his Holy Spirit indwelling us.

Empathy

Pastor's wives who are first-generation Christians are perhaps more surprised than anyone to be pastor's wives raising pastor's kids. In many ways it seems like a lifestyle pendulum swing. Whereas life in the fishbowl of ministry can appear far off from the realities of life outside of Sunday worship, the pastor's wife who did not grow up in a ministry or even Christian environment is uniquely relatable. She is aware of the ways of this present world beyond theory or observation, but with understandings that can only be obtained via lived experience. She understands the way the world thinks, craves, and drives itself into the ground. She has a deep empathy for the tension believers feel when praying for or interacting with unbelieving relatives or contacts.

The first-generation Christian pastor's wife is also assured that her faith is not fake because it was never delivered on a platter. Her faith must be hers without the bubble wrap, real and gritty, able to withstand the criticism of taking a different path than what she had been set on. The door was always open for her to walk away. She may have even been applauded if she had. Jesus had to be her only hope at the time when he was the only hope she had at all. This pastor's wife knows what every church guest is feeling, for she knows how it feels to step inside from the far outside. Even now among her relations, her Christianity might not be encouraged, or her ministry may be seen as unnecessarily fanatical.

Renewal

At the beginning of my marriage and my husband's pastorate, I thought I was prepared because I had been a Christian for several years, I loved God's Word, and I loved the church. I remember being so disappointed and angry at realizing how unprepared I felt at everything familywise. I used to get so frustrated that everything was new to me. Now I marvel at how God has made so many things new, from the ashes and fragments offered up in clueless, exhausted, embarrassed desperation.

You are a new creation in Christ, not a creation of your upbringing or background. You are new and are being renewed. In one generation, God can use you to break cycles that go back multiple generations. This is our God: he has made, is making, and will make all things new (Rev 21:1). In the day to day of your newness in Christ, as you encounter new lessons or tests, such newness is not a punishment. You have an opportunity to "learn to do good" (Isa 1:17) and to see first-hand the transformation that only God can do, in you and around you.

Whether you're a student, the wife of a student, or already serving in ministry, (or, Lord bless you, all the above), you know that churches can act like dysfunctional families. Where there are sinners, saved or not, there will be sins (Titus 3:3). Pastor's wives who grew up in particularly sinful environments might be just as surprised and critical as any to see imperfection in the church, but they are usually more prepared than most to witness it.

I have exactly zero memories of a time in my childhood that was not broken to the core, spanning from my earliest birthday through my legal age of adulthood. So, by the time I was a teenager, I could estimate almost precisely how many beers my alcoholic mother had had based on her telling behavior. Aggravated and stressed but not combative meant she had had one beer and was intent on another. A little too happy meant she had downed two beers. Singing loudly and urging me to dance with her was three-four beers. I knew that she was either at number five or finishing a six-pack when her face would contort into a grim anger that was suspicious of my attempts to help walk her to her bed. Negotiation skills became important after 6 or more empty cans could be counted. If I could get her to at least lie down before she became violent, I knew that her blood alcohol level would make it hard for her to be able to stagger back up to her feet. If I could accomplish this, the usual result was her sinking into a weepy depression on the couch or floor, which was miserable but lesser so than the alternatives.

Why share such a memory? It is not because I am proud of my negotiation skills, but to give an example of how personal experience with a troubled environment in its own way can prepare a heart of cooperation in the face of unreasonable choices and actions by others.

How could a mother - who should know and love better - put her child through such drama? How can a professing Christian – who should know and love better – put their church leadership or fellow members through such drama? This world is full of things that are not as they ought to be. And few people besides those who grew up amid dysfunction in such a household can so readily recognize and understand such dysfunction in a church and be able to approach it rationally without total shock at the sins of sinners. We don't enjoy it, and it never triggers happy feelings of familiarity. But we are less likely to be completely thrown by it. When conflicts arise in your church, you just might be the pastor's wife that is able to stay calm, especially if your background makes some church drama seem light by comparison to what you personally experienced growing up. Be careful not to let past difficulties (plus ministry) toughen your heart, and partner your calmness with tenderness.

It's often assumed that a background in ministry is the most blessed environment to grow up in for a future pastor's wife, with a broken home being the least blessed environment in the descending order of blessed backgrounds following a childhood spent in a pastor's home. If someone says, "I was blessed by God to grow up in a Christian home," am I then to say that "I was cursed by God to grow up in a non-Christian home?" Do the blessings described in Ephesians 1 apply to me or you any less than another child of God, just because we were raised in varied households? It *is* a blessing to grow up in a godly home, but those who grow up in other homes are not cursed, just blessed with different opportunities to see God's grace be sufficient and his power made perfect in much weakness (2 Corinthians 12:9). Nothing is wasted with God, and he gives first-generation Christian pastor's wives the ability to truly empathize with those in their church family who have also been through the wringer of this world.

Encouragements

"Seeing that His divine power has granted to us everything pertaining to life and godliness, through the true knowledge of Him who called us by His own glory and excellence. For by these He has granted to us His precious and magnificent promises, so that by them you may become partakers of the divine nature, having escaped the corruption that is in the world by lust. Now for this very reason also, applying all diligence, in your faith supply moral excellence, and in your moral excellence, knowledge, and in your knowledge, self-control, and in your self-control, perseverance, and in your perseverance, godliness, and in your godliness, brotherly kindness, and in your brotherly kindness, love. For if these qualities are yours and are increasing, they render you neither useless nor unfruitful in the true knowledge of our Lord Jesus Christ" (2 Peter 1:3-8).

Here are a few things I wish I knew before I became a pastor's wife that I hope will encourage you now.

1. Learn from God's Word and let him be your principal healer, teacher, and counselor. Note that I said "principal," as you can discerningly connect with other helpers and helps, but pay the

most attention to the Lord's leading and stay the most dependent upon God himself. Pray James 1:5-7, saying, "God I lack wisdom in..." He already knows it, but he might be waiting for you to come to know it and call on him with a humble, faithful, expectant posture.

2. First Timothy 3:2 describes a pastor as the husband of "one wife." God does not specify much about this one wife, and he is silent on her childhood background. Know that Scripture does not impose many of the subconscious qualifications that many do upon a pastor's wife, such as being raised in a Christian home or having attended seminary.

3. Pray hard for wisdom, encouragement, and his presence in the loneliness. As an introvert who was raised as an only child and latch-key kid, I was always comfortable being alone. However, as any introvert will tell you, being alone and feeling lonely are different experiences.

4. Something I wish I had done differently was to be honest with others about how difficult it was to learn. I wanted very much to impress others with how well-adjusted I was. I like to have it all together all the time. Don't be afraid to seek out support and mentors. Remember that the then pregnant virgin Mary went to visit her older cousin Elizabeth. You don't have to wait for someone to read your mind, you can and should make the first move if God is leading you. Though you are in a position of leadership, I would caution you not to keep your church family from investing in you. Remember that the early church frequently became family to the believers who were disowned by families of origin, both the Jewish Christians kicked out of synagogues and Gentiles ostracized by polytheistic society for following the one true God. You can learn from your local

church family and from brothers and sisters in the global church through countless resources available, just be discerning that it is all firmly rooted theologically in God's Word.

5. God tells is in James 3:2 that we *all* struggle in *many* ways. We don't need to pretend that we don't, or to believe anyone who pretends that they don't. Not only does every person struggle, but every person also struggles in many ways. My background was just one of many ways that I struggled. It may have been one way that branched off into other ways, but there are still other besetting flaws and deficits that may have less to do with my original household and more to do with my original sin. I used to look at others that had a godly upbringing and coddled the envious thought that they struggled less than I did. Yet if it's not one thing it's another. If it's not a familiar struggle to you then it's a different one that is familiar to someone else, and they probably wish it away as much as you wish yours away. You are human, and so is everyone else.

6. Psalm 88:12 reminds us that the darkness cannot know God's wonders and righteousness. Managing your own expectations of the sources and degree of support offered to you may keep you from being discouraged by criticism, resentment, or unsolicited advice about your approach to marriage, motherhood, or ministry.

Conclusion

The truth is that ministry can be a very scary-looking call for a woman who did not grow up in a ministry home, a Christian home, or even a functional home. Even truer, however, is that God knew you before He formed you (Jer 1:5). He knew the days in your childhood that you would experience leading up to your call into ministry (Ps 139:16). All of it was all appointed to you for that time (Eccl 3:1). This means that God knew exactly from where He was calling you to be wife to your pastor-husband and mother to your pastor's kids. He knew what he was calling you to step in and step up to. He began a good work in you, and He will be faithful to complete it (Phil 1:6).

I invite you not to be afraid to live out your Christian life in the real-time glass house of ministry, and to be strong and courageous, for the Lord your God is with you (Josh 1:9). Your church may be watching your every step, but God is ordering your every step. He is the one who sees you most closely and most purely. I invite you to persevere through the numerous headwinds and to enjoy the more numerous victories of witnessing God's sustaining grace and sanctifying power to make all things new in and around you. I invite you to treasure the good gifts of marriage and motherhood that God has given you.

If you always longed for a Christ-centered home, I hope that you will be blessed as your survey the opportunity that Christ himself has afforded you in building that home now. However, instead of applying perfectionistic pressure to yourself to build the home that you didn't have, I invite you to have nothing to prove to anyone, including yourself, about your capability to bless the Lord, your husband, and your children. Most of all, I invite you to feel as secure as God says you truly are, to rejoice and to relax in being sealed by the Holy Spirit in Christ. Know that God will never allow you to sink under the waves as long as your gaze is fixed on the author and perfector of your faith (Heb 12:2). May the Lord bless you and keep you sister, I'm rooting for you!

POURING FROM AN EMPTY CUP:
Soul Care for the Ministry Wife
Jennifer Gaddis

"The Lord is near to the brokenhearted and saves those who are crushed in spirit."
Psalm 34:18

I still remember the early days of being a new pastor's wife—my heart was full of hope and joy. I was eager to pour into everyone God placed in my path, to be a steady encourager for my husband, and to love our church family with open arms. I pictured a beautiful community marked by deep friendships and a shared passion for our sweet Savior. I imagined leading Bible studies, mentoring women, singing in the choir, teaching kids at Vacation Bible School, going on mission trips, working with students, leading conferences. The opportunities felt endless.

That's the image I had in my mind of what a pastor's wife was supposed to be. She was the paragon of hope, strength, and faith. She was a model of faith for the other women in the church. That was the kind of pastor's wife I longed to be. So, side by side with my husband,

I began pouring my heart and life into the lives of others. I poured and I poured, and I poured some more. It was a true surprise to me—though it should not have been—when I looked down one day and found my cup completely empty. I had nothing left to give. I found myself at a breaking point—though I didn't see it coming at the time. How did I get there? More importantly, what could pull me out of a season marked by spiritual depletion, emotional fatigue, and the relentless toll of always pouring out for others?

My Story

For 18 years, I had served alongside my husband, fully immersed in every aspect of life and ministry. I was a wife, a mom, and a caregiver to my aging grandmother. I led Bible studies, served in the worship ministry, homeschooled my little ones, and poured into the women of our church. My days were overflowing with meaningful ministry and good things. But somewhere, amidst it all, I realized I had wandered from my first love.

Without even realizing it, I had slowly faded from the closeness I once had with Jesus. I wasn't tending to my soul… or, more accurately, I wasn't allowing my Savior to tend to it. I entered a season of deep darkness. Nothing around me could fix it. My husband, Darren, as much as he tried, couldn't reach the ache. My children, precious as they were, couldn't lift the weight. Friends' prayers and encouragement didn't break through. Even quiet weekends away, meant for rest and reset, fell flat. Only Jesus could meet me there… but for a while, I didn't even want to try. Darren gently encouraged me to visit my friend, Mia, someone he thought might help—but I couldn't bring myself to go. I didn't want to leave the house, let alone go to church. I missed the joy I once lived with.

I remember the night it all came to a breaking point. Everyone in our home was asleep, but I lay wide awake, restless and empty. I didn't want to talk to anyone. I didn't want to be around people at all. That alone was foreign to me; I'm naturally a people person, joy-filled to my core, but that season had made me unrecognizable, even to myself. On that night, I quietly slipped outside onto our lanai, sat by the pool, and dipped my feet into the water. The darkness surrounded me, both outside and within. And then, suddenly, with tears starting to fall, I wept in a way I hadn't in months. I began to cry out, truly pleading to the Lord: "Jesus... I don't even know how I got here. I don't know how to get back. I'm tired. I'm overwhelmed. I'm exhausted. I'm empty. I'm heartbroken. I don't know what to do. Please, *please* help me." If someone had passed by our home that evening and overheard my sorrow, they might've thought, "That woman's lost her ever-lovin' mind."

It was in that moment of raw honesty and desperation that something beautiful happened: I was met by the undeniable presence of God. It was as if He sat right beside me, put His arms around me, and whispered, "Sweet girl, it's going to be okay. I'm here. I never left. This—right here—is where I want you. In my presence." That moment was the turning point for me. It was the beginning of my return. And no, my problems didn't all disappear overnight. The healing hadn't come in a sudden flash—but it began.

A few days later, a fellow pastor's wife reached out to me unexpectedly. I barely knew Liz, but a friend's mom had shared with her that I was going through a hard season. She felt led to call. Looking back, I know it was a divine appointment. I had already convinced myself I was depressed, thanks to too much time seeking an answer online. Liz had a different diagnosis. She gently said, "Sweet girl, you're not depressed. You're burned out."

When Liz identified my problem as burnout, I was reminded of Martha, along with her sister Mary, and how I—without realizing it—

had chosen the path of busyness over intimacy. I had replaced stillness at His feet with endless running, serving, giving, counseling, and doing. All were good things, but none of them were Him. I had been giving everything I had to others without allowing myself to be filled first.

Liz also encouraged me to shift my gaze from my circumstances to the one who reigns sovereign over them. "He will fill you," she said. "He will give you everything you need to return to the place of intimacy with him. Pray, even when it doesn't feel like he's listening, because he is. Read the Word, even if nothing sinks in, because it will. Lean in. He'll meet you there."

She also encouraged me to surround myself with friends who would intercede without judgment, who would walk with me, and who would remind me of truth. It was through that community that God did indeed encourage my heart. My dear friend Amanda (herself the daughter of a pastor) walked closely with me through that season. She listened with compassion, encouraged me when I couldn't find the words myself, and created a safe space where I could be completely honest—no filters, no fear of judgment. Just grace.

At the time, I had no idea why the Lord was allowing such a painful, dry season, but now, I can see it clearly. He was refining me, teaching me, and molding me into the woman He could use for His purpose and glory. Since then, I've had the privilege to sit across from countless women—many of them walking through similar seasons. And I've been able to say, with full assurance, "I understand. I've been there. You're not alone. And Jesus will meet you here, too.

Choose What is Better

> "Mary has chosen the good portion,
> which will not be taken away from her."
>
> **Luke 10:42**

Mary and Martha's Story

If there was such a thing as a poster girl for pastors' wives, Martha would likely be at the top of the list. Like so many ministry wives often do, she was constantly serving—always giving, always pouring herself out.

In Luke 10:38-42, Jesus visits the home of Martha and Mary. Martha, the host, is busy with preparations, serving, cleaning, making sure everything is "just right." Meanwhile, Mary sits at Jesus' feet, listening to His teaching. Frustrated, Martha comes to Jesus and says, "Lord, do you not care that my sister has left me to serve alone? Tell her then to help me!" To this, Jesus gently responds, "Martha, Martha, you are anxious and troubled about many things, but one thing is necessary. Mary has chosen the good portion, which will not be taken away from her."

Faithfulness Isn't Busyness

Martha's work was good. The hospitality, service, and effort were all wonderful things. But Jesus reminds us that being busy for him is not the same as sitting in his presence. Sometimes we can be so caught up serving and trying to be a faithful servant for Jesus that we forget to simply sit with him. We need to remember Psalm 46:10: "Be still and know that I am God." Before we can pour out into others, we must be filled by him. Our ability to love and to teach others flows from our intimacy with Christ, and ministry begins by being deeply rooted in him. He is the source of our strength.

Prioritize Presence

We are all called to do good works, but presence with the Lord should be first and foremost in our lives. For this reason, perhaps Mary is one whom pastors' wives should most aspire to be like. Mary chose to sit at Jesus' feet—a posture of closeness and humility, a heart ready to listen and learn from him. That is what Jesus says is "better." He wasn't dismissing service but reminding us of what nourishes the soul first. Our serving should begin with our abiding in him. We serve better when we start by sitting with him.

As the psalmist proclaims, "One thing have I asked of the LORD, that will I seek: that I may dwell in the house of the LORD all the days of my life, to behold the beauty of the LORD and to meditate in his temple" (Ps 27:4). My heart should long for nothing more than Christ for He is my everything. He is the one who fills me up.

Jesus Cares About Our Heart

Jesus addressed Martha's anxiety and frustration directly. He saw her stress, not just her service. His correction was tender, not harsh nor shaming. He invited her to slow down. God doesn't just want the work of our hands; he wants our hearts at rest in him. He wants to spiritually nourish us as we learn from him, and he offers to us fellowship with him over worldly tasks and responsibilities. This is true rest. Rest for your soul. A deep, sustaining peace.

Matthew 11:28-29 says, "Come to me, all who labor and are heavy laden, and I will give you rest. Take my yoke upon you, and learn from me, for I am gentle and lowly in heart, and you will find rest for your souls."

Choose What Is Better

Jesus said, "Mary has chosen," implying we also must choose the better portion. Rest, stillness, and time with Jesus often go against the grain of our worldly culture and ministry life, but they are essential. Time with Jesus isn't optional nourishment—it's the one thing completely necessary. The story of Mary and Martha is a gentle but powerful invitation: "Come, sit. Be with me. Learn from me. Trust me. Experience peace in me. Live for me." This is especially important when we're exhausted, depleted, or burned out. Jesus reminds us, "You're worried about many things... but only one thing is truly needed."

When Your Soul is Tired

> "Come to me, all who labor and are heavy laden,
> and I will give you rest."
>
> **Matthew 11:28**

We all face seasons where we feel worn thin, stretched by responsibilities, consumed by expectations, spiritually exhausted. Even when we're doing good things—serving others, raising families, serving in various ministries—our souls can grow tired. I know this personally. I've lived it. And maybe, just maybe, you're living it right now. But here's the truth: Jesus never asked us to do it all on our own. He invites us to come. To sit. To be still. To be filled.

In my journey into and back out of physical, emotional, and spiritual depletion, I have learned some biblical yet practical ways to press into God when you feel like pulling away, when your soul is tired. These are not worldly formulas, they are truths taken from God's Word. They are lifelines for when your spirit is dry and your heart is weary. These exhortations have helped me consistently return to the source of my strength.

1. Keep Your Eyes on the One Who Guides You

When burnout clouds your vision, it's easy to fixate on your circumstances. Hebrews 12:2 urges us to "fix our eyes on Jesus, the author and perfecter of our faith." Remember, he is the one writing your story. Don't let fear, fatigue, or frustration become your guide. Keep looking up. Even when you don't understand what he's doing, trust that he knows where he's leading you.

2. Keep Praying

You may not feel like praying—but don't stop. Talk to God even when the words feel hollow. Cry out when all you have is tears. Prayer isn't a performance; it's a posture of surrender. As Paul encourages us in 1 Thessalonians 5:17: "pray without ceasing." Stay connected to him. Keep the conversation going.

3. Stay in God's Word

When life is overwhelming, the enemy will whisper, "You're too busy. You're too tired. The Word won't help." But that's when you need God's Word the most. If God is the one who is writing your story, it is in his Word where you'll learn who he is. You'll also be reminded of who you are in him. The Scriptures are your source of truth in a world filled with noise. "Be still and know that I am God" (Ps 46:10).

4. Stay Connected to God's People

Don't isolate yourself. When you're exhausted or discouraged, it is tempting to retreat, but healing often comes through community. Let others carry you in prayer. Let them encourage you and speak life into you. Remember, faith is not a solo sport; God designed us to walk together. "Encourage one another and build one another up" (1 Thess 5:11).

5. Keep Confessing and Repenting

Spiritual depletion can expose hidden sin: pride, self-sufficiency, bitterness. Don't ignore it. Bring it into the light. When sin is identified, repent and turn away from it. As the wife of a pastor, you may feel the pressure to always present yourself and your family as "having it together" and never in need of correction or improvement. Do not see confession as a shame to be avoided; it is a freedom to be enjoyed. As 1 John 1:9 promises, "If we confess our sins, He is faithful and just to forgive us and to cleanse us from all unrighteousness." Do not deprive yourself of the blessing of confessing where you fall short. It is out of the kindness of God that he leads us to repentance (Rom 2:4).

6. Pursue Him Relentlessly

It is not easy to lean into spiritual things when feelings of doubt, weariness, or disconnection creep in. It's hard to attend church activities in such times. My advice is to keep showing up and keep pursuing Jesus with all that you have, even when you feel nothing. Don't base your faith on feelings—they change. God doesn't change. Your pursuit of him isn't about striving, but about surrender. He meets you in the seeking. "You will seek Me and find Me when you seek Me with all your heart" (Jer 29:13).

7. Keep Serving (But with the Right Heart)

Serving others is a gift, but if you're running on empty, it can become a burden. Serve from a place of overflow, not obligation. It's also helpful to remember that you are not the Savior; Jesus is. Serve with joy, not performance. Serve with dependence, not pressure. Serve because you get to, not because you have to.

8. Keep Worshipping

Worship may seem easier when our world is right, but it is most beneficial when things seem amiss. Job worshiped in the midst of his suffering (Job 1:20-21). David worshiped as he fled from Saul (Ps 34). Habakkuk rejoiced in the Lord in midst of scarcity (Hab 3:17-18). Paul and Silas sang to the Lord in prison (Acts 16:25). It is always a good time to worship the Lord. Worship resets your soul. It reminds your heart of who God is and what he's done. Even in your weariness, lift your hands. Lift your voice. Worship your way through the darkness. "God is our refuge and strength, a very present help in trouble" (Ps 46:1).

9. Keep Gathering with Other Believers in Corporate Worship

You need your church family—and they need you. Don't give up on being with your brothers and sisters in Christ. As Hebrews 10:25 reminds us, even when you don't feel like going, press in. There is power in gathering with the saints. There is power in sitting under the preached Word. There is power in an encouraging word. There is power in your shared faith with other believers.

10. Take Your Thoughts Captive

Burnout often begins in the mind before it displays itself elsewhere. Lies take root and spiral into discouragement. As a counter to the discouraging thoughts, Scripture commands us to "take every thought captive and make it obedient to Christ" (2 Corinthians 10:5). Speak truth over your emotions. Let God's Word regularly wash over you. His revealed truth is more reliable than your feelings.

A Final Encouragement to You

Burnout doesn't mean you're weak. It doesn't mean you've failed. It simply means you've been pouring yourself out—and now it's time to let Jesus fill you again. If you find yourself in a depleted season and your cup is empty, don't rush back into the busyness. Don't walk away from the stillness. Stay near to the Lord. Let His presence become your dwelling place, not just a place you visit when you're desperate. Mark 12:30–31 reminds us of what matters most: "AND YOU SHALL LOVE THE LORD YOUR GOD WITH ALL YOUR HEART, AND WITH ALL YOUR SOUL, AND WITH ALL YOUR MIND, AND WITH ALL YOUR STRENGTH. The second is this, 'YOU SHALL LOVE YOUR NEIGHBOR AS YOURSELF. There is no other commandment greater than these."

There's a reason he tells us to love him first. When our love for God is our priority—when we pursue him with our whole heart—he fills us in a way nothing else can. And from that place of fullness, we're able to love and serve others not with our own strength, but with his. That is the sweeter place, the better portion, the life-giving nourishment your soul is longing for.

So breathe. Rest. Return to Jesus. Let Him fill you—and stay close.

Many blessings to you, my sweet sister in Christ. May the fullness of Jesus overflow in your heart, and may you live each day with unwavering passion, clear purpose, and a deep awareness of his presence. May he propel you to be his hands and feet in this world, and may you stand firm—steadfast and bold—in the gospel of Christ.

MAKING FRIENDS IS ALWAYS WORTH IT
Tiffany Burgner

When I was a little girl, my parents went through a divorce. That event would go on to shape the rest of my life in ways I never anticipated. At such a young age, feelings of rejection and abandonment crept into my heart, taking root in a way that would remain with me for many years. Although I know that the Lord has redeemed those broken parts of me with His grace upon grace, the emotional scars of that time have had a lasting impact. They have shaped who I am today, especially in how I relate to people. One of the most significant effects of that experience was the deep and unrelenting desire to be loved and accepted.

As a teenager, I found that friendships became one of the places where I could find a sense of love and belonging. Being surrounded by friends, knowing they cared for me and would not abandon me, brought me immense joy. It was in these friendships that I first began to realize how important loyalty and deep connection were to me. I also knew that I wanted to be the kind of friend who could give that same love and support in return. One of the friendships that deeply resonated with me was the one between Anne and Diana in *Anne of Green Gables*, by Lucy Maud Montgomery. Anne, an orphan who had spent much of her life in and out of various orphanages, yearned for a "bosom friend" — someone who would love her unconditionally and stand by her side through all of life's ups and downs. As I navigated my own life and friendships, this longing for a deep, steadfast connection became something I cherished.

As I grew older, the Lord blessed me with an answered prayer. He brought me Aaron, who would become my best friend and the love of my life. We met in 10th grade, dated through high school, and married a few years after graduation. Aaron had felt a call to full-time vocational ministry when he was 17, and I knew when we married that I would be a minister's wife. The thought of joining him in ministry was both beautiful and exciting to me, and we jumped into this journey with hearts full of hope and expectation.

Dare to Make Friends

For the first part of our ministry, Aaron and I moved every three to four years, as God called us to new places of service. These transitions, while difficult, were always accompanied by the assurance that we were right where God wanted us to be. However, moving was never easy, because we quickly grew to love every single place God called us to minister. In particular, I always felt incredibly thankful for the friends he placed in my life to walk through those seasons with me. God did this in every place he sent us. In one place, the friend was the wife of the senior pastor; in another, it was the wife of the chairman of the search committee that had brought us there. In still another, it was a church member who shared with me how much she appreciated our friendship, and how, with her, I could be myself without any pressure of ministry expectations. Each one of these women was a unique gift from God and each one has been invaluable to me. I still hold them close in my life today.

However, there was an aspect of ministry I hadn't prepared for — the inevitable loss of friendships. There are many voices in the ministry world, and some of these voices caution against forming close friendships with people in the church, particularly if you are a pastor's wife. "You'll get hurt if you get too close," some people say. Other voices encourage pastor's wives to dive in and form godly, deep friendships within the church, because those are the relationships that will last for eternity and bring great joy today. At various pastor's wives' events, I've heard it strongly recommended to seek out these friendships, as they are considered one of the greatest blessings of ministry. I chose to listen to that second set of voices, to make friends in the church. I encourage you to do the same, even though that first set of voices is right, you can get hurt.

I am so grateful for every friendship God has blessed me with in our ministry, but nothing could have prepared me for the pain of losing a friend because they decided to leave our church. Before that happened, I had always been the one leaving; leaving places I loved because God was leading us elsewhere. Those kinds of losses, while painful, were bearable because I knew that no matter the distance, my friends knew how much I loved them. They would always be a part of my life. However, when the loss came not because I was leaving, but because a friend was walking away, it was far more difficult to bear. When someone I had loved and walked alongside chose to leave for reasons unrelated to me or my ministry, it stung in a way I hadn't expected. Whether they left because they found a church they thought would better fit their needs, or they left because they were angry with else in the church, it was still hard not to take it personally. It felt like a resurfacing of those old feelings of abandonment from my childhood. But making friends is always worth it.

Don't Build Walls

For me, it would be easy after experiencing the loss of a friendship due to ministry to put up walls. The easy thing for me would have been to say that I am not going to allow myself to be vulnerable again or allow myself to get close to people because they will inevitably hurt me. I actually have this thought in my mind from time to time, but I know it is rooted out of fear and hurt.

This is why I must go to God's word for guidance, rather than living on the basis of feelings. These are the moments when we must cling to God's word more than ever and trust Him. Yes, even in Scripture the Apostle Paul experienced rejection when his friend Demas left him (see Col 4:14; Phlm 24; 2 Tim 4:10), but that did not stop Paul from moving forward in ministry. It did not stop him from making friends.

We have a gallery wall in my house that my husband and I love. You can see it right when you walk in, and we love to show it to people when they are first visiting our home. We call it our "ministry journey wall." At the top of the gallery is a picture of our wedding day and a wooden plaque that says, "Aaron and Tiffany established 2000." Underneath that plaque are 8x10 photos of the churches where we have served. This wall is like our "stones of remembrance," reminding us that God is always faithful, that he will never leave us or forsake us. Every time we look at those pictures, it is so clear to us that the Lord has us on a journey. A journey we could have never imagined when we first started dating in high school. One of the best parts of that journey has been how we have met so many amazing people over the 25 years of full-time ministry, and how through those people we have experienced so many blessings. Our wall gallery reminds us that sometimes there is change, and that sometimes with that change will come loss, but those changes also bring new beginnings and new people Don't put up walls in your life that will keep you from experiencing the blessings God can bring through others.

God is Always Gracious

If you have experienced the loss of friendship, remind yourself of God's faithfulness to you (Heb 10:23). Show grace to those who have hurt you, recognizing that bitterness is poison to your soul (Heb 12:15). Allow yourself to be vulnerable. After all, nothing is greater than love (Mark 12:31). Yes, with great love comes opportunity for great hurt. But with great love also comes opportunity for great blessing. Be encouraged. We serve a good God who will one day make all things right, even our broken relationships Make friends, it's always worth it. Trust him.

TODAY YEARS OLD

Monique N. Igbinoba-Cummings

❖❖❖

I nervously held my husband's hand and walked with him from the church office to the church sanctuary on a sunny day in June 2001. The day my husband was installed as lead pastor of our church I was a 28-year-old newlywed. The sanctuary was filled with pastors, ministers, church members, family, friends, community members, and guests. As we were led down the left aisle of the sanctuary to the first row, I smiled with each person that made eye contact with me. My husband's installation service was a beautiful whirlwind. Each carefully selected scripture and encouraging word exhorted my husband to be steadfast and unwavering in his love for the Lord. He was encouraged to stand for Christ, love his family, and shepherd the people he was called to serve. I remember thinking to myself, "Wow, that's a lot."

As for me, I was encouraged to be a helpmate to my husband and an active supporter of his ministry. I was encouraged to love the people he was called to shepherd, to serve the church community, to be an example of a biblical wife, and to maintain a healthy home life, all while growing in my own faith. To be transparent, the "encouragement" shared with me at my husband's pastoral installation seemed more like a list of expectations for any pastor's wife. I wondered about the list of "encouragements," because, unlike my husband, I wasn't on staff at our church. Yet, it was presumed that I would, without hesitation, take on a role that had specific expectations. As each speaker "encouraged" me, no one referenced my lack of experience or that I hadn't formally "applied" for the role. When I look back at the pictures taken during my husband's pastoral installation, I see a 28-year-old newlywed pastor's wife, filled with excitement and uncertainty at the same time. I would have to learn to deal with expectations, feelings of inadequacy, and loneliness, eventually arriving at a place where I could both give and receive the blessings of ministry.

Expectations

Rather than just dipping my feet in the water, I jumped into the journey of serving as a pastor's wife with both feet. I actively supported my husband's ministry. I supported and worked with every ministry at our church—literally, every ministry. I passed out flyers, greeted people as they entered the church, helped with the children's ministry, taught a small group Bible study, cooked for our annual food extravaganza, monitored the bounce house during church festivals, addressed graduates for our baccalaureate service, camped with our church girl scout troop, counseled new wives and moms, edited the church newsletter, and planned women's ministry activities (just to name a few!). Of course, I didn't do all these things at once, but they often overlapped.

Amidst the busyness of ministry, I still didn't realize the profound impact my husband's call to the pastorate would have on my life. The pastor's wife was expected to know everything related to the church. The new time for choir rehearsal, the location of the extra paper towels, and the schedule of Vacation Bible School activities were just a few of the items I was expected to have at the ready. It took a while, but I learned I didn't have to memorize all the information printed in the church bulletin or commit every announcement made from the platform to memory. My role as a pastor's wife began to impact the way I viewed the wives of other leaders. Imagine the thought of reaching out to the wife of your children's elementary school principal to ask if the new school budget might support additional field trips, even though she wasn't a part of the school staff.

I quickly learned I would regularly be identified by my husband's job/calling. I was usually introduced as "the pastor's wife." My actual first name didn't seem all that important. As with the beginning of any journey, my experiences began to craft how I viewed my role as a pastor's wife. The "wow, that's a lot" feeling I had for my husband on the day he was installed as pastor had been added to my role as well. Would I be an effective pastor's wife?

In addition to the support I provided to the various ministries and church activities, I literally stood next to my husband each week, smiling and talking with every church member and guest that came through our end of service receiving line. I was blessed to hear lots of "life snippets." Sometimes I shook hands, sometimes I clasped both hands with my own, or sometimes I hugged someone's neck. I was always careful to follow their lead. I never wanted anyone to feel uncomfortable. I wanted everyone to feel they had my full attention. I listened with my ears and heart. Our end of service receiving line often became an impromptu counseling session. I relished the opportunities to talk and walk with church members as they shared their excitement about new relationships, new jobs, new babies, graduations, weddings, retirements, and the like. Their excitement to share with me warmed my heart. Although daunting, I also embraced the part of my role that required me to walk with others through the ending of relationships, relocations, and loss of family and friends.

I spent a great deal of time coming alongside others and never took for granted any of the dozens upon dozens of relationships I was blessed to cultivate. Dealing with the emotional rollercoaster of the highs and lows of others was difficult and, at times, overwhelming. I prayed for balance between my role as a pastor's wife and my identity as a woman of Christ, a wife, and a mom. Coupled with my own life "life-ing," my journey as a pastor's wife led to the perfect storm of feelings of inadequacy and loneliness.

Inadequacy

How could a pastor's wife feel inadequate? How could I feel inadequate in a role given to me by God? How could I feel inadequate when so many trusted me with their triumphs and insecurities? I sometimes found myself waiting on the sidelines as things happened in our church community secretly hoping that I wouldn't have to get into the game. I didn't know it then, but I learned, over time, the true impact of the wholly unrealistic pastor's wife expectations placed on me by others (as well as the expectations I had placed on myself). I watched seasoned pastor's wives attend every worship and prayer service, plan and organize women's ministry and mission trips, assist with church-wide activities, manage their families, and be an example of a Proverbs 31-woman year after year—a fierce provider and protector for those she cares about. I wondered if life was "life-ing" for seasoned pastor's wives like it was for me. Would I ever be a "seasoned" pastor's wife?

The demands of life, at home and at church, overwhelmed me and I began to feel inadequate. The wise Proverbs 31 woman who excelled as a wife, a homemaker, and an industrious businesswoman seemed far beyond my reach. The feeling of inadequacy was a slow, steady burn. I didn't know what to do, but I knew I had to do something. I prayed for guidance, and with the support of my husband, I stepped back from some of my most demanding ministry responsibilities. I learned that my listening ears and heart were taking in too much. My mind, body, and spirit were tired.

Philippians 4:11 reads, "Not that I speak from want, for I have learned to be content in whatever circumstances I am." I learned that God doesn't always change what we're going through, but he can, and he will, change how we see things. I didn't realize I was conflating admiration and comparison as I watched seasoned pastor's wives. I learned that admiration did not have to lead to emulation. As much as I'd love to say the admiration/comparison/emulation lesson was learned quickly, it wasn't. Slowly, my feelings of inadequacy were replaced with an appreciation for my individuality as a pastor's wife. Focusing on the role God crafted just for me as a pastor's wife renewed my mind, body, and spirit. I felt a sense of encouragement and confidence that allowed *me* to be *me*.

Loneliness

In addition to feelings of inadequacy my journey as a pastor's wife was sprinkled with feelings of loneliness. I've heard many stories about ministry loneliness, and I've also experienced it firsthand. It's hard to explain the irony of being lonely in ministry when there's a church full of people eager to have a relationship with the pastor's wife. Unfortunately, the eagerness to have a relationship was sometimes directed toward the role of the pastor's wife rather than me as a person. It can be hard to function in a space that doesn't always see you as an individual. At times, it was hard for me. My husband's calling to stand before the congregation every week didn't mean I wanted too as well. Relationship expectations were very high. Imagine having someone you barely know ask for your phone number or give you their phone number and ask when you can chat. Being a pastor's wife is one of the few roles where you are expected to be a friend to everyone, whether they are a friend to you or not.

I was years into my journey as a pastor's wife when I learned it was okay to decline dinner invitations, birthday party invitations, etc. I prayed for a discerning spirit when invitations were extended or when I was approached by potential friends. As I learned to move and walk in the space God set for me, the pressures that led to loneliness began to slowly dissipate. I was able to cultivate godly relationships within our church and with other pastor's wives. I was able to share without fear of being judged. I found acceptance as a member of our church that no longer had to be "super spiritual" or "perfect."

Eventually, the pressures I had allowed to frequent my role as a pastor's wife no longer tipped the scale to loneliness. I slowly found the balance that worked for me. I let go of the pressure to be the perfect sister in Christ to everyone. It was too much. I learned that meeting others at the point of their need didn't mean my own needs had to be neglected. Loneliness was no longer par for the course. Although I sometimes still feel like I live in a fishbowl, God has provided opportunities that have granted me the confidence to form relationships with fellow sisters in Christ and pastor's wives. Ministry loneliness is no longer a burden.

Give and Take

My journey as a pastor's wife provided opportunities to walk alongside others as they faced some of life's most difficult circumstances and decisions. The Bible makes it clear that our walk with Christ is not meant to be smooth sailing—our struggles help to refine us. I am blessed to be able to seek the Lord on behalf of others, often praying for compassion and grace. Some difficult circumstances and decisions shared with me have been hard to hear and process, but I am thankful that God has allowed me to see others as He sees them.

I've experienced a rollercoaster of emotions during my journey as a pastor's wife. At one point, I experienced going from the exhilaration of learning about a new baby in our congregation to deep sorrow upon learning about another family's loss of a child, all within the span of a couple of hours. I learned to be intentional about not injecting myself into the difficulties and burdens of others because their difficulties and burdens are not about me. I learned that absorbing the emotions of those around me led to me being emotionally exhausted. I'd love to say that emotional exhaustion is no longer a thing, but I am, of course, a work in progress—and I'm okay with being a work in progress. I know that God is actively involved in my life. He's not done with me yet.

I don't take lightly that I am trusted to walk through difficult circumstances and decisions with fellow sisters and brothers in Christ. Although I recognize the importance of walking with others through trying times, I have often walked through my own difficult circumstances and decisions alone. Other than my husband, I have struggled to allow others to walk alongside me. I am, by nature, a caregiver and the thought of burdening others and receiving help has always been hard for me to accept. At times, being a pastor's wife has heightened this feeling, but I am happy to say that I now see how others are blessed to walk alongside me just as I am blessed to walk alongside them.

Second Corinthians 1:3-4 reads, "Blessed be the God and Father of our Lord Jesus Christ, the Father of mercies and God of all comfort, who comforts us in all our affliction so that we will be able to comfort those who are in any affliction with the comfort with which we ourselves are comforted by God." I know God's comfort has surrounded and protected me over and over and over. I know He has provided comfort for me so that I may provide comfort for others. Allowing others to walk alongside me has changed my ministry perspective and deepened many relationships. I'm now living a life filled with godly "give and take," mirroring the teachings and example of Jesus as shown in Galatians 5:13, that we are "to serve one another in love." As I look at my journey as a pastor's wife, I have been blessed to minister alongside my husband, share the love of Christ, see lives transformed, maintain a healthy home for my family, walk with others through difficult circumstances and decisions, and share and receive compassion and grace. I'm grateful for my ministry journey, and how it has helped to shape me and grow my faith. I am blessed to have connections filled with compassion and grace because both are needed to build and reinforce relationships. I have learned the importance of self-reflection, and it has become an important part of my spiritual growth.

In years past, when I set out to be strong and not burden others, I didn't realize that by denying others the opportunity to walk alongside me, I was being selfish. It may seem counterintuitive, but a serving heart can also be a selfish heart. My serving heart was selfish because I only allowed compassion and grace to flow in one direction—from me to others. I often told myself that it was better to give than to receive. In my zeal to serve others, my actions had placed me on a path focused on pleasing people rather than pleasing God. You're probably wondering how serving others could be turned upside down. It was easy to convince myself that serving others was a good thing to do because it was and it is. No way could good intentions produce selfish results, but they did. I learned a lesson that changed my life; compassion and grace are two-way streets.

Conclusion

Through my journey as a pastor's wife, I've learned to serve and be served, to grant myself the same compassion and grace I grant to others. Self-reflection through prayer has helped me to push beyond the feelings of inadequacy and loneliness and embrace the roles I've been blessed with—woman of Christ, wife, mom, and pastor's wife, to name just a few. Romans 12:2 reads, "And do not be conformed to this world, but be transformed by the renewing of your mind, so that you may prove what the will of God is, that which is good and acceptable and perfect." While I've been a pastor's wife for nearly half my life, I'm okay with "today years old" lessons that help me to focus on being a God pleaser and aligning my life and roles with his word and will. The list of "encouragements" shared with the 28-year-old newlywed pastor's wife doesn't seem so daunting now. A godly perspective is key. My journey continues with a renewed mind, body, and spirit. Yours can too.

TWO CALLINGS, ONE COVENANT:
Tending the Garden Together
Jennifer Duncan

It is a deep honor to have been invited to contribute to this work. I approach the topic of being a pastor's wife with humility, aware of the many faithful women who have walked this road far longer than I have. Although I often feel I have little to offer, I recognize that each journey, no matter how brief, holds value. In my 31 years of life (with only a handful of those spent in ministry), this is my humble offering, an invitation into my "garden" and what the Lord has been teaching me along the way.

Tending the Garden

As I prayed and sought the Lord for direction on what to write, I found myself reflecting on the importance of titles, their weight, their beauty, and the honor they carry. Titles have a way of shaping how others see us. They communicate our roles, responsibilities, and place within relationships. In some cases, titles speak louder than names. Scripture reminds us how important titles are. For example: servant, prophet, priest, and king. Each of these titles signifies not only a role, but a calling from God. The Scriptures teach us that Jesus himself bore many titles: Son of God, Son of Man, Lamb of God, Messiah, Friend of Sinners, Savior. Each one of these titles reveals something essential about who he is.

One of the earliest titles we encounter in Scripture is "helper." In the book of Genesis, we see that God's design for marriage was intentional and purposeful. When he created Eve and gave her to Adam, he called her an *ezer*. This is the Hebrew word for helper. In the original language, this word means strength, support, and aid.[2] It indicates a shared responsibility. This suggests that Eve wasn't an afterthought. She was always a part of God's plan in redemptive history.

Eve was a vital partner to Adam. She was equal in value yet distinct in her role. Genesis teaches us that God placed Adam in the garden to tend to it, and then he created a suitable *helper*, Eve, to aid him in that work. This title given to Eve is holy and divine. In her book *Being God's Image: Why Creation Still Matters*, Carmen Joy Imes says, "*ezer* is not a demeaning label, it is most often used for God himself," emphasizing Eve's calling as a vital partner from the very beginning of creation.[3] This role reflects the nature and character of who God is. Eve's example provides a model for women to actively participate in and contribute to God's mission. God gave Eve both a title to embrace and a place to serve. In a sense, each of us have been entrusted with the task of tending a "garden."

The Garden of Eden wasn't only a place of paradise and perfect harmony, it was also a place given to Adam and Eve to care for,

---

[2] Katharine C. Bushnell, *God's Word to Women*, ed. and rev. by Ray Munson (Dallas, TX: Bible Study and Research Centre, 2003), 21.

[3] Carmen Joy Imes, *Being God's Image: Why Creation Still Matters* (Downers Grove, IL: IVP Academic, 2023), 27.

cultivate, and steward. They were to do this work together. This meant they were to prune the garden, protect it, and cultivate life from its soil. As I began to write and meditate on these things, God used that imagery as a powerful metaphor for how I view life and calling in ministry. The life of marriage and ministry resembles the same rhythms of tending a garden. It requires work, nurture, care, grace, and patience. Some seasons are filled with blooms, good fruit, growth, and beauty. Other seasons require pulling weeds, pruning, cutting what's overgrown, or digging deep into the soil. Some days the sun is shining, other days there are looming clouds. What I have come to learn is that all these things are necessary in tending the garden. God gave Adam and Eve this task prior to the fall in Genesis 3. We are to see this work as necessary and rewarding. We all have a garden to tend to, and, in this case, it is my marriage and ministry.

This garden metaphor brings fresh perspective to the title "pastor's wife." We are not merely standing beside our husbands who carry the calling; we have been called, too. We are co-laborers, cultivators, and fellow gardeners in the soil of gospel ministry. God has given each of us the necessary tools and a sacred ground to tend. Our work may not always be seen by others around us, but it is always seen by God. This work is not always in the spotlight, but it is in the soil, and I have found it is there that God does his deepest work. While we focus on what we see above ground, God sees what is beneath the soil.

Identity

There have been seasons where I have felt like my whole identity was tethered to my husband's work, and in a lot of ways, it is. I am a part of him. However, there are times I have felt my identity gets lost behind the title "pastor's wife," as if my name only exists in connection to his. In many ways, I treasure that and see it as a sacred

TWO CALLINGS

thing. Therefore, I do not want what I just said to diminish the sacredness of the role, but I want to be honest and name what most feel they cannot say. I love walking beside my husband in this calling, but at times it can also feel isolating. There is this unique tension in being honored in the role yet experiencing an ache to be seen or known for who I am beyond it. In those moments, I cling to the truth that God knows me fully and that He calls me by name. He has given me a purpose that is both deeply connected to and uniquely distinct from the man I love.

Women in this role often feel unseen and unheard. We are frequently the ones in the shadows managing the home, juggling the children, and coordinating meals, appointments, extracurricular activities, and bedtime routines, often while maintaining a full-time job. There are dishes waiting to be done, laundry that needs to be folded, and little souls to be poured into. Some days it feels like there aren't enough hours in the day to take care of yourself because the demands are so high. I say this knowing there are wonderful pastors and fathers who share in these responsibilities, and I am married to one of them. I am speaking specifically to the unspoken expectations.

Long after the pastor leaves the office, he comes home, and we find ourselves continuing to pour out. We tend the wounds left by careless words from a church member, speak truth over our husbands when they are ready to throw in the towel, and remind them that God has called them. We hold space for the heartache when business meetings go downhill, when families grieve, when division threatens the church. Ministry doesn't end at the sanctuary doors. It follows us into the kitchen, the nursery, the living room. We carry it quietly, yet faithfully, and often tearfully. And when the sun sets, and we are hours away from doing it all over again, we lay the burdens of the day at the feet of Jesus and, through it all, we keep tending and we keep contending. We water what is weary, prune what is necessary, and trust God with the growth.

Expectations

There are seasons in ministry when, as a pastor's wife, you can be surrounded by people yet feel deeply alone. It is easy to believe you must always be strong, always "on," and never let your guard down. Friendships can feel complicated. While some put you on a pedestal, others keep their distance, unsure how close they can get. There are certain relationships or titles in life, like mother or father, that come with silent, almost universally understood expectations. No one has to explain that a parent should care for, nurture, and provide for their child. It is just understood. It is expected that a mother will comfort, a father will protect, and that both will sacrifice in ways that often go unseen. These roles carry built-in responsibilities that are often felt before they're ever spoken, and they shape how we move and serve within them.

One of the most challenging aspects of being a pastor's wife is not always found in what people say, but in the unspoken expectations they carry. You are expected to be at every event, every meeting, every funeral, every wedding, and if you are not, it feels like you've fallen short. There is a pressure to know everyone's name, even though few remember yours, and so you become "the pastor's wife." And heaven forbid you run to the grocery store on a Saturday afternoon in sweats and no makeup, only to bump into a church member who comments on your appearance, as if not only your presence but also your presentation must always meet a certain standard. These expectations are real, and somehow, we are meant to carry them with grace and joy.

Balance

I began attending the Baptist University of Florida in the fall of 2014, pursuing a Bachelor of Arts in Missions. At the time, I was convinced I would remain single and pursue a long-term career with the International Mission Board. I had my eyes set on the journeyman program and the nations. I have always been strong-willed, and those who know me might even say stubborn, so when God brought Caleb into my life, I resisted because I already had my life planned. As Proverbs 16:9 reminds us, "The mind of man plans his way, but the LORD directs his steps."

Caleb and I met on August 14, 2014, and our very first conversation was about missions. He, too, was pursuing a degree in that field. We married two years later on April 16, 2016, in the R.G. Lee Chapel on campus at the Baptist University of Florida. After graduation, we both worked at the university before continuing our education at Southeastern Baptist Theological Seminary. I pursued a Master of Divinity in Missiology, and Caleb earned a Master of Arts in Ethics, Theology, and Culture. During our final year of seminary, we learned we were expecting our first child. Our son was born on September 10, 2020, right in the middle of a global pandemic. I graduated that December, and Caleb graduated the following semester in May of 2021.

Our story doesn't follow the usual script, and I've come to see that as a gift. While I do carry the title of pastor's wife, I also bear a unique calling of my own. God placed a burden for ministry on my heart years ago, one that began on a short-term mission trip to Nicaragua in 2013 and came full circle seven years later when I stepped into full-time ministry at First Baptist Chipley in October 2020. The timing did not make sense to the world; we were in a pandemic and had a newborn, but the Lord had prepared the soil for a new season, and He called me to plant anyway. It was a season full of challenge and change, but also deep joy.

I continue to serve on staff at First Baptist Chipley as the Executive Assistant to our pastor, as well as the Director of Women's Ministry and Missions. It is by God's grace He allows me to use my gifts and education to serve the local church. Caleb and I are still learning how to walk this road, not just as husband and wife, but as co-laborers in the garden God has entrusted to us. We don't always get it right. Some days we forget to water. Some days we grow weary. Yet even in those moments, we learn, we grow, and we trust the Lord to provide the increase.

Our story is unique in that we are both in full-time vocational ministry. Caleb serves as the Associational Missions Strategist for the West Florida Baptist Association, where he faithfully supports and serves the churches in our region. He often steps in as an interim pastor or fills the pulpit if a pastor is out of town. As a result, we are not always physically serving side by side on Sunday mornings. While he pours into one congregation, I remain rooted in our home church: leading, supporting, and ministering to the women God has placed in my care, whether through formal roles or volunteer service.

It is never easy. There are mornings when I am dressing the kids, packing a bag, and getting them out the door so Caleb can study, pray, and prepare to preach elsewhere. Sometimes, before he can make it back home, I have already fed the kids lunch and laid them down for naps. Then I ask myself if I should do the laundry, read a book, or try to get a nap myself. The list of to-dos is endless. Caleb and I have learned not to let unspoken expectations take root. Instead, we honor each other's roles, share the load as best we can, and offer grace for the seasons that feel more like plowing than planting. It is not always a perfect balance, but it is the garden God has given us, and we are committed to tending it together.

Boundaries

Practically speaking, we have learned the importance of setting firm boundaries to protect what matters most. While Caleb's role often requires him to be away from our local church, we have made it a priority to worship together several Sundays out of the month. That rhythm is deeply important to both of us, not just for our own spiritual connection, but for our children as well. We want to worship together as a family. We desire our kids to experience structure, to grow up rooted in a local church they know and love. We are also learning to be intentional about safeguarding our time together. Boundaries are not a bad thing, and we have learned the beauty of saying "no" to good things to protect our time together. Like a garden, our marriage requires constant care and nurturing. What this looks like in our home varies from season to season. Some evenings we may read a chapter in a marriage book together, ask intentional questions about each other's day, read the Bible and pray, or watch one of our favorite shows. On other nights we are so spent we go straight to bed and wake up to do it all over again. Our marriages directly impact our family and the health of our ministries. I realize that protecting our covenant is not selfish; it is divine stewardship.

We have also learned, (sometimes the hard way), that rest does not happen by accident. It must be pursued with intention. There was a season when our Sundays were full from start to finish. We would serve at church in the morning, come home for a quick two-hour break, and then I would leave for my discipleship group. Two hours later, we'd swap: Caleb would take the kids, and I'd come home just as he was heading to his group. These were good things, holy even. But we began to realize that our constant going was stealing the little time we had to simply be together as a family. So, we made a change. We moved our discipleship groups to different days of the week, and in doing so, reclaimed Sunday afternoons as sacred time to rest, reconnect, and enjoy the gift of each other. We've learned that rest is not laziness, but obedience, and a way we honor God and each other.

Sometimes, others try to tend our garden for us by offering unsolicited advice, comparisons, or criticism, as if they know better how to cultivate what God has entrusted to us. Other times, we might be tempted to step into someone else's garden, measuring our growth against theirs or trying to prune what is not ours to touch. The truth is, each of us has been given a unique plot of soil to steward, with its own challenges and seasons. To flourish, we must stay focused on the task God has set before us, guarding our hearts against distraction and comparison. When we keep our eyes on the Master Gardener and diligently tend our gardens, we allow him to work through us in his perfect timing and way.

A Sacred Calling

I know the role I carry is sacred. It is weighty and at times lonely, but I know I am not unseen. I am not just "the pastor's wife." I am a woman called by God, planted with purpose, equipped with strength, and entrusted to tend the garden He's placed me in. I know I must anchor my identity in that reality because that is the identity that holds me steady when all others feel uncertain. There are days when the labor feels hidden, but I trust that none of it is wasted. Because Genesis 3 happened, this garden now cries out with us; it resists and groans, and the work can be laborious and wearying. I am reminded of Psalm 121, "I will lift up my eyes to the mountains; from where shall my help come? My help comes from the LORD, who made heaven and earth." As we serve as *ezers* in this calling, let us be encouraged that our ultimate help is not found in ourselves, but in the One who planted us, God, the Maker of heaven and earth.

While I was recently visiting Crater Lake National Park, I had the chance to hike through a peaceful meadow full of wildflowers and running streams. I remember being inundated by this thought: no one comes out here to water these flowers. No gardener stands watch with a hose to make sure they get the proper amount of water they need. No human effort sustains their beauty. God had already made provision for them. He renders the rain to fall, the streams to flow and the earth to yield. Everything within my view was thriving without striving. It reminded me that the same God who tends to those wildflowers is the one who tends to me. He knows what I need. He sustains the work he's called me to. Even when my own garden feels overlooked or weary, I can trust that he has already made provision for its flourishing.

Every quiet act of service, every prayer whispered in the dark, every time I choose faithfulness over comfort, it all matters to him. With each season, I feel my thumb getting a little greener, growing in wisdom, patience, and grace as I learn to tend this garden with more care and trust in him. So, I'll keep tending. I'll keep trusting. And when the seasons feel long and the soil seems unyielding, I'll remind myself that this is not the end. One day, my earthly titles will fade. The expectations, the constant pouring out, and the unseen work will all cease. And I will find myself in a new garden, where I no longer have to till or prune or strive. There, in the presence of the Master Gardener, I will be fully known, fully restored, and finally at rest. Until then, I will remain faithful in the garden he has given me, joyfully sowing, patiently waiting, and always growing.

THE BIBLICAL CALLING OF THE PASTOR'S WIFE

Gary L. Shultz Jr.

Introduction

I met my wife, Kristin, at church the Sunday before beginning my last year of college. If it wasn't love at first sight, it was close. I saw her for the first time during the service, sitting on the other side of the sanctuary with some friends from school, and elbowed the friend next to me when we were supposed to be singing. "We need to make sure we introduce ourselves to those girls before they leave!" Kristin and I started dating a few weeks later.

In those early days of our relationship, getting to know each other, we talked a lot about calling. We were both at Baptist Bible College in Springfield, MO, and we both knew that God was calling us to specific ministries. I was there studying to be a pastor and, maybe one day, a professor teaching others how to be ministers of the gospel. I knew I was headed to seminary next, and then wherever God would take me.

THE BIBLICAL CALLING

Kristin was there because she was called to be a teacher, and she wanted a Christian education to help her prepare to do just that. She had come halfway across the country to study at Baptist Bible College, at the recommendation of her pastor and church. She didn't know exactly where God might take her, but she was open to anything, including missions work overseas. I was immediately attracted to her strong sense of calling and desire to serve God. But there was one big problem. She wasn't sure she was called to be a pastor's wife.

Our school had gotten the nickname, "Baptist Bridal College" because people would joke that many young ladies would attend just so they could marry a pastor. That was not her. And if I was called into pastoral ministry, and she was called to something else, how was that going to work? But at the same time, we clearly liked each other, and it seemed to us that God was in that too. Was God calling us to one another? And if God was calling us together, did that mean our callings were compatible? Or did that mean one of our callings would need to change?

In addition to talking and praying through these questions, I also began to investigate what the Bible says about callings, and how we should understand them. We eventually came to realize that if God was calling us to one another, then he was calling us into ministry alongside one another, however that might look. So that meant that he was calling Kristin to be a pastor's wife (and me to be a teacher's husband!). As we will see, the Bible refers to several "callings" for each person, and each one is meant to complement the other as we all live our lives with and for God in Christ by the Spirit. Praise God he faithfully equips us to fulfill the callings he gives us through both our ministries and our marriages!

There is no doubt that the call of the pastor's wife is a unique one, bringing together calls in work, family, and the church in ways that no other call does. Because of this, it can also be a challenging one, because it is often lived out amidst unspoken expectations and little specific direction. This makes it vitally important to understand exactly what the Bible does and doesn't say about calling, and this calling in particular. While the Bible never specifically mentions the calling of "pastor's wife," it does say enough about calling to give us some clear guidance. In the rest of this essay, we're going to explore what the Bible says about calling. God calls us to himself in Christ, and then he calls us to particular vocations, our marriages and family roles, and to our particular churches and places. Once we've established that foundation, we'll then think through how that understanding relates to the specific calling of the pastor's wife. Putting all this together will help clarify expectations about this wonderful calling, give us some specific direction about how to fulfill it, and, I pray, assist you in experiencing this calling as a blessing, just as God intends.

Calling and Salvation

The Bible has a lot to say about calling, especially when it comes to our calling as Christians. For example, the wonderful promise of Romans 8:28, that God "causes all things to work together for good to those who love God," immediately clarifies that those who love God are those who are "called according to his purpose." The next verse then explains what this purpose is, that God intends for those he calls to be "conformed to the image of his Son," or to become like Jesus. In other words, those whom God calls in this way are Christians, those who are chosen, justified and glorified in Christ (Rom 8:30). Calling in this passage is an act of God the Father that brings us into his family in Christ by the Spirit. God assures us in his

Word that when he calls us to himself, he completes his work of salvation in us.

The rest of the New Testament elaborates upon this theme of calling in relation to our salvation. For example, in 1 Thessalonians, Paul thanks God for the Thessalonians because their faith demonstrates that God has called them to himself through the gospel, that they would gain "the glory of our Lord Jesus Christ" (1 Thess 2:13-14). In his letters, Peter reminds the believers to whom he is writing that God has called them "out of darkness into his marvelous light" (1 Pet 2:9), to the Father's "eternal glory in Christ" (1 Pet 5:10), by God's "own glory and excellence" (2 Pet 1:3). We're also told that those called by God to salvation are "of Jesus Christ" (Rom 1:6) and "saints" (Rom 1:7; 1 Cor 1:2). We're reminded that believers are called to experience God's peace (Col 3:15), hope (Eph 1:18), sanctification (1 Thess 4:7), freedom (Gal 5:13), and eternal life (1 Tim 6:12), all in the context of a relationship with God the Father in and through Jesus Christ (1 Cor 1:9).

Therefore, we should think of calling as God's authoritative summons to his children to accomplish his purposes in their lives. The Holy Spirit personally addresses believers through the Word of God, and as believers hear the Word in the power of the Spirit, they hear the voice of God and choose to follow it. As Jesus reminds us in John 10:27, his sheep hear his voice, are known by him, and therefore they follow him. This happens first and foremost in salvation, as we become new creations in Christ (2 Cor 5:17).

Calling and Work

While our call to salvation is the predominant idea when the Scriptures speak of calling, it is not the only one. The Bible speaks of several other callings in a person's life. How 1 Corinthians talks about calling helps us to see this. As he opens this letter to the church in

Corinth, Paul reminds the Corinthians who they are in Christ. He states, "Paul, called as an apostle of Jesus Christ by the will of God, and Sosthenes our brother, to the church of God which is at Corinth, to those who have been sanctified in Christ Jesus, saints by calling, with all who in every place call on the name of our Lord Jesus Christ, their Lord and ours" (1 Cor 1:1-2). The Corinthians are those who are "sanctified in Christ Jesus" (set apart to be holy in Christ), and therefore "saints by calling," the same as all those everywhere who "call on the name of our Lord Jesus Christ." This is the calling to salvation that the Bible emphasizes. In Christ, we are all called as saints, holy ones set apart to Jesus Christ through our confession of faith in him.

However, in this introduction Paul not only reminds the Corinthians of their calling as believers, but he also reminds them of his own calling as an apostle. Paul had been called as "an apostle of Jesus Christ by the will of God." Paul's calling as an apostle was bound up with his conversion (see Acts 9:1-20), but it wasn't the same thing as his conversion. All Christians are called by God to salvation, but only Paul was called by God to be his chosen apostle to the Gentiles (cf. Gal 1:15-16). Throughout 1 Corinthians, Paul refers to his unique calling several times, especially as he tries to convince the Corinthians that they themselves, through their transformed lives in Christ, bore witness to his calling as an apostle to preach the gospel to them (1 Cor 1:17; 4:15; 9:1-2; 15:9-11). God's will was for Paul to serve him and the Corinthians in this specific way.

What this means is that God not only calls us to salvation, but to particular works, or vocations (the English word "vocation" comes from the Latin word for "calling"). We often speak this way when we talk about someone being called to ministry as a pastor or missionary or even a pastor's wife. However, the Bible leads us to understand that every job, career, or work (whether paid or unpaid) is a calling, and not just vocational ministry. When God created humanity in his image and likeness, he commanded humanity to "subdue" or "rule" his creation in his stead, as unto him (Gen 1:27-28). We see this happen right away with Adam in Genesis 2, as God puts Adam in the Garden "to cultivate and keep it" (2:16), or to work! Work has been corrupted by our fall into sin (Gen 3:17-19), but it is something that all human beings are designed to do by God and unto God. God calls every one of us to particular works.

We often live as if what we choose to do with our lives is all up to us. We start asking our children at a young age what they want to be or do when they grow up, encouraging them to make certain choices toward those ends as they get older. We assess our own personalities and interests, taking career inventory tests, choosing whether we want to go to college and what we might want to study (or whether we want to marry a pastor and be a pastor's wife or not!), all to the end of figuring out what we want to do. However, as Christians, we should always be asking God what he wants us to do, what he is calling us to do. God in his gracious providence gives us particular interests, gifts, personalities, opportunities, circumstances, and callings to work and serve in specific ways. God called Paul to be an apostle. He calls some to be pastors. He calls some to be teachers, or doctors, or police officers, or social workers. He calls some to start their own businesses, or to serve without pay in volunteer roles (Paul was not always paid as an apostle, he sometimes had to make tents to support himself, Acts 18:3). He calls some to work primarily within the home. He calls some to be pastors' wives. All of this is according to his will. We should consider every work we perform in light of God's calling and desire.

Calling and Family

The call to specific kinds of work is not the only other call we see in Scripture, however. Staying in 1 Corinthians, we find Paul speaking of God's call in another way in 1 Corinthians 7, the calling of family. This chapter is full of practical instructions on marriage: the responsibilities husbands and wives have toward one another regarding marital intimacy (7:1-7), whether or not people should get married or stay single (7:8-9; 25-38), divorce (7:10-16), and remarriage (7:39-40). Amidst these instructions, Paul validates them theologically in terms of "assignment" and "calling." In 7:17, he states, "Only, as the Lord has assigned to each one, as God has called each, in this manner let him walk. And so I direct in all the churches." That is, God calls us to himself (saves us) in different circumstances, which he has "assigned" to us.

Paul's overall point is that no matter our circumstances, no matter our places, and no matter our positions, we can serve God in and through them. We don't necessarily have to forsake them or seek to change them when are saved, because they are all part of his calling on our lives. Some of us are called to salvation when we are single, and some of us are saved when married. Some are saved as circumcised Jews, some are saved as uncircumcised Gentiles (7:18-19). Some are saved as slaves, some are saved as free people (7:21-22). Regardless of what circumstances we are in when we are called to salvation, they have been assigned to us by God, according to his will. They are part of our calling.

To be a husband or a wife is to be called by God to be a husband or a wife, to the spouse he has given us. Just as our callings to specific works are grounded in the wonderful truth of God making us in his image and likeness, so too are our callings in our families. When God created humanity, he created us "male and female," to "be fruitful and multiply, and fill the earth" (Gen 1:27-28). Just like with work, we

THE BIBLICAL CALLING

see this aspect of our calling right away in Genesis 2, when God declares that it is not good for Adam to be alone, demonstrates that none of the animals he created are suitable partners for him, creates Eve from Adam's side, and calls them together as husband and wife (Gen 2:18-25). And just like with our work, our martial relationships and commission to fill the earth are corrupted by sin (Gen 3:16). But just as human beings are still designed and called to work despite sin, too are human beings still designed and called to be married (though not every individual human being will be called to be married, as 1 Cor 7 reminds us). And the calling of marriage leads to the rest of the family callings we might experience, such as being called as mothers, fathers, daughters, sons, sisters, or brothers. Many of us have several of these callings at once (for example, God has called me as a husband, father, son, and brother). All these callings are assigned to us by God.

As we often assume that the work we choose to do is all up to us, so we often assume that whether we choose to be married or not, or even remain married, is up to us. However, as Christians, we must recognize that God is the one who calls us to marriage. If we are married, it is God in his gracious providence who has led us to our spouses. If we are married, it is God in his gracious providence who has called you to be married to this exact person. If you have been called to marry a man who is called to be a pastor, God, in calling you to marry this man, has called you to be a pastor's wife. This is true regardless of your background, education, spiritual gifts, or anything else about you or your circumstances. And if God has called you, he is faithful to equip you to fulfill your calling.

We should also note that our callings in the family and to specific vocations do not contradict one another, any more than they contradict our foundational callings as Christians. All of us have multiple callings in different realms. Perhaps God has called you as a pastor's wife, a mother, a daughter, and to work in a specific vocation outside of the home. This will no doubt be overwhelming at times (we know that everything is affected by sin), this will no doubt be misunderstood at times (we know that everyone is affected by sin), but the promises and goodness of God to help you fulfill your callings still hold firm. Consider again Paul's instruction in 1 Corinthians 7. In 7:22-23, Paul encourages those who are slaves when they become Christians to remember that they ultimately belong to God, and therefore even in their bondage they are free in him. This doesn't mean they should resign themselves to their lot in life; it means the gospel frees us to fulfill our callings, even hard ones, as unto God, knowing that he is with us, that he never leaves us or forsake us (Heb 13:5-6). All your callings, including your calling as a pastor's wife, come from God, and he means for all of them to fit together for your flourishing.

Calling and Place

There is one final aspect of calling we should consider before we bring everything together. When God calls us to himself and gives us particular callings in our families and vocations, he always does so in particular places. Consider 1 Corinthians 1:1-2 one more time. Those called by God to be saints were "the church of God which is at Corinth." This is one of those details in the Scripture that is easy for us to overlook because it seems obvious. Of course, a local church only exists in a particular place. Of course, a letter to a local church must then be written to a particular place. But where a local church is located matters. In writing to Corinth, Paul addresses particular issues to particular people in a particular place with a particular context. When he writes to those in Rome (who are also called as saints, Rom 1:7), he addresses different issues to different people in a different place with a different context. Where God puts us, our places, are part of our callings. They are not an accident.

THE BIBLICAL CALLING

All people are shaped by their places, by their cultures and social contexts. God also means for us, as his people, to influence the places in which he has put us—our countries, communities, neighborhoods, homes, and churches—so that people may be shaped for his glory and their good. Even as God saves us and therefore calls us to be citizens of his coming kingdom (cf. Col 1:13), he calls us to live out our salvation, our kingdom life, in specific places in this world. We also see this aspect of calling in Genesis 1-2. When God creates Adam and Eve, he places them in the Garden (Gen 2:9). It was this specific part of God's good creation they were to fill and subdue, in which they were called to work and to be a family. Yes, sin impacts our place just as it impacts our work and our family (we know Adam and Eve were expelled from the Garden). But part of God's calling on our lives is to be faithful believers right where he has placed us, to make disciples as we go, knowing that he will be with us wherever we are, until the end of the age (Matt 28:18-20).

This calling of place is intimately tied to the calling of our church. The Corinthians were called as the "church of God" in Corinth. When God saves someone, they become part of God's people everywhere and for all time, "a chosen race, a royal priesthood, a holy nation, a people for God's own possession" (1 Pet 2:9), but we can only live this truth out with actual people in an actual place as part of a specific church. Each church member has been called by God to be part of their church, gifted to benefit a specific body of Christ, called to reach their neighbors and nations through the mission work of a specific congregation (1 Cor 12:12-20; Acts 13:1-3).

Yes, just as we often assume we choose our own work and families, so too we typically assume it's all up to us where we live and where we go to church (or if we go to church). Yet if these aspects of life are also callings, we must also approach them from God's perspective, asking him where he wants us to be, where he wants us to go, and which church he wants us in. This is especially important for pastors, who are also church members, but church members with formally recognized vocations and responsibilities within the church (Acts 6:4; Eph 4:11-16; 1 Tim 3:1-8). If God has called you as a pastor's wife, he has called you to be a church member and a pastor's wife in a particular congregation in a particular place for a particular time. He has called you to the congregation that he has called your husband to pastor. He has gifted you in a particular way for the needs and benefit of your congregation. He has not placed you where you are by accident. Your church is a key part of how he is working together all things for good in your life.

Calling and the Pastor's Wife

The calling of a pastor's wife involves every aspect of God's calling. God calls you first and foremost to himself, to be his child. He calls you to be a wife to your husband. He calls you to a particular church. He calls you to work and serve in various ways. While every calling is different from every other calling, there are specific things we can say about what this should look like in your life, based not only on what we understand from Scripture, but on the cultural expectations that often accompany this role as you strive to live it out. Let's consider three areas our understanding of calling impacts: the pastor's wife's ministry to her husband, the pastor's wife's ministry to her church, and the truth that the pastor's wife is not the pastor.

The Pastor's Wife's Ministry to Her Husband

Every church has a slightly different job description for their pastor, and every church has different expectations for their pastor. However, there are certain things a pastor is supposed to do no matter what church he is in, because the Bible commands them. A pastor should preach, teach, pray, lead, witness, serve, and shepherd. These things take time and effort, often more time and effort than a pastor has in a given day or week. Even more importantly, these things require a deep and meaningful relationship with God if they are to be done well. This means the ministry of a pastor's wife to her husband is essential to his ministry.

The stronger a pastor's marriage is, the stronger his ministry can be. His relationship with God, and therefore his ministry, will not be stronger than his marriage. All Christian marriages are meant to be living pictures of the gospel (Eph 5:22-33), which means if the pastor is going to have an effective ministry, fulfilling all his varied responsibilities before God and for his church, his marriage must be what it should be. Do your best before God to love your husband, to treat your home and your family as your first ministry. Prioritize your marriage. In God's call to you as a pastor's wife there will be nothing that will impact the effectiveness of your husband's ministry, and therefore the spiritual health of your church, more than your relationship with him (and the same is true for your husband's relationship with you).

The Pastor's Wife's Ministry to Her Church

If a pastor is married, there are certain aspects of his calling he will only be able to do well with his wife's help. For example, a pastor is commanded to be "above reproach" (1 Tim 3:2), which means that in his ministry to women he will sometimes need your help, even it only involves sitting by his side as he counsels or visits someone. A pastor is commanded to be "hospitable," (1 Tim 3:2), which means that in welcoming the stranger or opening up his home he will sometimes need your help. A pastor is commanded to "manage his own household, keeping his children under control with dignity" (1 Tim 3:4), which means he will need your help as you parent together.

As you think of the works and the ministries in the church to which you have been called, consider how you can help support and strengthen your husband's ministry. God has called you together, and your husband needs your help. Remember that as God's callings, these works will present themselves to you in accordance with your opportunities, gifts, and desires. But sometimes God will give you new gifts and desires to meet new opportunities. Remember too that these works will never contradict or overthrow your other callings, and that there are some seasons of life when you will be able to do things you aren't able to do at other times. For example, empty-nesters have more time for others than mothers of small children, and God knows that.

A Pastor's Wife is Not the Pastor

Finally, my encouragement to you in light of the biblical truth of calling is to remember that the pastor's wife is not the pastor. This is one of those statements that even in writing it I can't help but think, "Duh! Of course the pastor's wife is not the pastor! She's the pastor's wife!" But I still believe it needs to be said, because I've been married to a pastor's wife for over twenty years. My wife has never confused her role with mine, but I have seen how many church members have. People dissatisfied with something I've said or a decision I've made have gone to her instead of me. People with suggestions about a new ministry have made them to her instead of me. People have asked her to change something I'm doing instead of asking me. So together, we've always done our best to model the biblical truth that the pastor's wife is not the pastor. She has gotten very good at graciously saying, "Please talk to Pastor Gary about that!"

In calling you to be a pastor's wife and not the pastor, God has called you to be your husband's wife, to share in his ministry, and to be a faithful church member, not to fulfill his role, even if asked. I hope you experience this as freedom. Your calling should be defined and determined by God, not by the expectations or demands of others (not even by the expectations or demands of yourself!). Participate in the ministries God to which God has called you, not the ones to which he called previous pastor's wives. Don't feel guilty if you miss a church event to stay home with a sick child. Rest in your calling.

Conclusion

First Timothy 3:1 tells us that if a pastor aspires to the office, it is a fine work that he desires to do. This has always been a reminder to me that for all its unique difficulties, the calling of a pastor is a wonderful calling (and it is!). The same is true with the calling of the pastor's wife. If God has led you to marry a pastor, it is a fine work to which he has called you. May you know the power of his presence and the goodness of his love for you as you live this calling for him.

LIST OF CONTRIBUTORS

Tiffany Burgner has a B.A. in Social Sciences from the University of South Florida and has recently written her first children's book, *You Can Be Brave Too*. Tiffany has served alongside her husband, Aaron, who has served in full-time ministry for the last 25 years. She currently resides in Lakeland, Florida, where Aaron has served as the Senior Pastor of Lakes Church for the past eight years. She enjoys the day-to-day blessings of being a mom to two amazing children, a wonderful daughter-in-law, and one precious grandson.

Jennifer Duncan has a B.A. in Missions from Baptist University of Florida and an M.Div. in Missiology from Southeastern Baptist Theological Seminary. Jennifer currently serves as the Executive Assistant to the Pastor and Ministry Director for Women's Ministry and Missions at First Baptist Church in Chipley, Florida. She is married to Caleb Duncan, who serves as the Associational Mission Strategist for the West Florida Baptist Association and Assistant to the Dean of the School of Theology and Ministry at Baptist University of Florida. They have served in full-time ministry together for five years and have two children, Hunt and Hope.

Jennifer Gaddis has devoted more than twenty-five years to women's ministry. She and her husband, Darren, Senior Pastor at First Baptist

Church of Ocala, have been married for over twenty-eight years and are blessed with three children: Leah (Zach), Ethan, and Meredith.

In 2023, Jennifer served as President of the Southern Baptist Convention's Ministers Wives Luncheon. Currently, she serves on the board of One More Child and as the Executive Human Resources Director for Chick-fil-A in Ocala, Florida. Her greatest joy is pointing others to Christ while faithfully balancing her callings as a wife, mother, leader, and servant of God.

Monique Igbinoba-Cummings is a speaker, consultant, and educator. She is a two-time graduate of Howard University, where she earned a B.A. and M.Ed. She also earned a Ph.D. in Educational Leadership from Lynn University. Monique serves as the Women's Ministry Director at New Life Church in Miami, Florida, where her husband Erik serves as the Lead Pastor. They are the grateful parents of Reaiah and Erik II. As a family, they enjoy biking, playing outdoor schoolyard games, all things Disney, and watching Jeopardy.

Seana Reavis is an epidemiologist by training, but a pastor's wife by calling. She has served in ministry for 20 years alongside her husband Josh, who is co-pastor at North Jacksonville Baptist Church in Jacksonville, Florida. Together they are the proud parents of Anna Rose, Abraham, and Shepherd.

Liz Traylor, a native of Alabama, resides in Pensacola, Florida, where her husband, Dr. Ted Traylor, has been the pastor of Olive Baptist Church since 1990. As a speaker, she conveys truth with humor as she teaches Bible studies and speaks at events for women of all ages. A creative writer, Liz has contributed to devotionals and textbooks, written abundant scripts for church drama, and produced curriculum for her church. Since becoming a grandmother, Liz has returned to preschool ministry and a call to refreshed priorities: her Lord, her family, and Sunday dinner around her table.

www.ingramcontent.com/pod-product-compliance
Lightning Source LLC
Chambersburg PA
CBHW060408050426
42449CB00009B/1935